THE THROWS

Contemporary Theory, Technique and Training

4th edition

Edited by Jess Jarver

TAFNEWS PRESS

Book Division of Track & Field News, Inc.

First published in 1994 by Tafnews Press
Book Division of Track & Field News,
2570 El Camino Real, Suite 606,
Mountain View, California 94040 USA

First edition printed in 1974
Second edition printed in 1980
Third edition printed in 1985
Fourth edition, with all-new material, printed in 1994

Standard Book Number 0-911521-35-6
Printed in United States of America

Cover design and production: Teresa Tam

PHOTO CREDITS

Cover	Tony Washington	All-Sport/Gray Mortimore
7	Patrick Boden (1989 NCAA)	Bill Leung, Jr.
19	Ruth Fuchs	Fionnbar Callanan
33	Petra Felke	Horstmüller
35	Jason Wyatt (1993 NAIA)	Heinz Ruckemann
46	Brian Oldfield	Zigurds Mezavilks
52	Christy Barrett (1991 TAC)	Victor Sailer/Agence Shot
63	Pam Dukes (1988 TAC)	R.M. Collins III
74	John Powell	Jeff Johnson
83	Igor Nikulin (1990 Goodwill)	John Giustina
93	Tore Gustafsson	Kevin R. Morris
105	Yuriy Syedikh	All-Sport/Simon Bruty
111	Silke Renk (1989 WUG)	Horstmüller

TABLE OF CONTENTS

Chapter I: General Principles

Chapter II: The Shot

Chapter III: The Discus

Chapter IV: The Hammer

Chapter V: The Javelin

ACKNOWLEDGEMENTS

The publishers wish to thank the following publications for their cooperation and permission to reprint articles that originally appeared in their pages.

Athletics Coach, Malcolm Arnold, Editor. Published by the British Athletic Federation, Edgbaston House, 3 Duchess Place, Hagley Road, Edgbaston, Birmingham B16 8NM, England.

Australian Track and Field Coaches Association Seminar Report, Rothmans Foundation, 309 Kent Street, Sydney, NSW 2000, Australia.

Der Leichtathlet, Peter Gran, Editor. Published by Deutscher Verband für Leichtathletik der DDR, Dimitroffstrasse 157, Berlin 1055, German Democratic Republic. (Now ceased publication.)

Die Lehre Der Leichtathletik, Helmar Hommel, Editor. Published as part of *Leichtathletik* (see below).

Legkaya Atletika, 103021 Moscow K-31, Rodjeatvensk Bulvar 10/7, Russia.

Leichtathletik, Heinz Vogel, Editor. Published by Deutscher Sportverlag Kurt Stroof GMBH, Eintrachtstrasse 110-118, 5000 Köln 1, Germany.

Modern Athlete and Coach, Jess Jarver, Editor. Published by Australian Track and Field Coaches Association, 1 Fox Avenue, Athelstone, S.A. 5076, Australia.

National Strength & Conditioning Association Journal. Published by National Strength & Conditioning Association, 300 Old City Hall Landmark, 920 O Street, Lincoln, Nebraska 68508, USA.

New Studies in Athletics, Bill Glad, Helmar Hommel, Bjorn Wangemann, Editors in Chief, published by IAAF Publications Department, 17 Rue Princesse Florestine, MC 98000 Monaco.

Odaviske Tehnikast, by Hans Torim. Published by Pedagogical Institute, Tallinn, Estonia.

Revue de l'AEFA, Daniel Lamare, Editor. Published by Association des Entraineurs Français D'Athletisme, 10, rue du Faubourg-Poisonnère, 75010 Paris, France.

Teoriya i Praktika Fizicheskoy Kultury, V.K. Balsevich, Editor. Published by Teoriya i Praktika Fizicheskoy Kultury, 18 Kazakova, Moscow, Russia.

Track & Field Quarterly Review, George G. Dales, Editor. Published by the NCAA Division I Track & Field Coaches Association, 1705 Evanston, Kalamazoo, Michigan 49008, USA.

Track Technique, Kevin McGill, Editor. Published by Track & Field News, 2570 El Camino Real, Suite 606, Mountain View, California 94040, USA.

CHAPTER
GENERAL
PRINCIPLES

SPEED AND POWER-ORIENTED TRAINING OF YOUNG ATHLETES

by Dr. Gudrun Lenz and Dr. Hans-Jürgen Frolich, Germany

The distribution of various training methods in the multifaceted development of young throwers in the 13 to 14 years age range.

The main aim in the training of young athletes is a multifaceted development of their basic athletic potential that is transferred through well planned training into a specific level of performance for a particular age group. This allows an early identification of real talent and avoids the variability inherent in evaluation based on past championships successes. Making an assessment of young throwers based purely on championships results has led to discrepancies in systematic load increases. The multifaceted development approach promulgates a rational distribution of general and specific training means and emphasis between technical and conditioning training.

Consequently, the following tasks are applicable to the planning of training for young athletes in the throwing events:

- Development of general and multifaceted performance capacities: speed, jumping, power, general throwing capacities, general strength capacities and endurance. The development of strength capacities involves all muscle groups with the aim to improve power and at the same time reach a sufficient level of maximal strength and strength endurance.

- Development of general and multifaceted coordination capacities: improvement of basic techniques in all track and field events, as well as other sports, such as games, gymnastics, swimming, winter sports and the like.

- Development of specific coordinative capacities: improvement of technique in the four throwing events combined with the initial development of specific throwing capacities and weight training techniques.

The final target is well expressed by Rost (1989) in:

- a multifaceted and age correspondent development of biological functions and

- a highest possible development of neuromuscular coordination and widely varied sports skills.

Creating favorable conditions for the development of speed and power requires methodical placement of emphasis in the training processes on these complex capacities together with technical and coordination development tasks. Training should be focused to:

1. Develop a model structure of the competition movement that is in time-space and dynamics close to the structure of the planned eventual target model. This is achieved by using implements that allow the athlete to reach delivery velocities and distances that correspond to the target performance.

2. Employ all training means in regulated volumes that are not excessive for athletes in this age group yet adequate to assure a satisfactory specific conditioning level for performance.

3. Structure effectively the conditioning, learning and complex microcycles to assist the motor learning processes and, in particular, the development of speed and power.

THROWING TRAINING

The emphasis is placed on:

- the employment of multifaceted general and specific throwing forms with different coordination demands

TABLE 1: PRINCIPLES OF A METHODICAL USE OF THROWING EXERCISES IN THE TRAINING OF YOUNG (13- TO 14-YEAR-OLD) THROWERS

General throws: different implements, different delivery actions and different positions (medicine balls, tennis balls, cricket ball, batons, stones, etc.; one hand, both hands, forward, backward, sideways; hitting, pushing, slinging; standing, kneeling, sitting; standing position, with a runup, rotating, etc.)

Specific throws: throws with the regular (competition) implements (shot, discus, javelin, hammer) and throws with lighter than regular implements and assisting devices.

	Mesocycles		
	1 - 3	4 - 5	6 - 7
Emphasis on:			
General throws	xxx	xx	xx
Regular implements	x	xx	xxx
Lighter implements	xxx	xx	xx
Number of throws in a training unit:			
General throws	50-80	75-100	50-80
Regular implements	—	10-15	10-15
Lighter implements	10-15	15-20	15-20
Weekly frequency	2-3	3-4	3-4

Method: General throws—5 to 8 repetitions in a series with 2- to 4-minute recoveries.
Specific throws—5 to 8 repetitions in a series with 1- to 2-minute recoveries between single attempts, 5 to 10 minutes between series.

(different weight and mass implements).

- an explosive and powerful movement structure in all throwing exercises.

- an optimal pretension created by an active use of lower extremities (legs).

- a conscious start of the delivery movement by the legs, particularly when lighter implements are used.

- a systematically increased load (implements) that corresponds to the explosive strength and power qualities of the athlete (see Table 1).

STRENGTH TRAINING

Emphasis is placed on:

- relatively uncomplicated exercises that young athletes are able to control and master aimed at developing explosive power characteristics.

- a load range that allows for the fastest possible execution of the exercises (30 to 50% of the maximum in sets with 3- to 5-minute recoveries in between).

- changing of the execution conditions (for example, joint angles) to vary the exercise in order to facilitate an explosive performance. This also applies to exercises against the athlete's own body weight (see Table 2).

SPRINT AND JUMP TRAINING

- Sprint and jump training must contain the coordinative technical demands of an intensive speed and power performance.

- Starts over short distances (10 to 30m) from different positions (standing, crouch, etc.) and with different starting signals, hurdle sprints over hurdles of various heights spaced at various intervals, as well as slightly downhill sprints, offer the maximal development possibilities.

- The same applies to single-leg, and in particular double-leg, takeoffs in jumping exercises to develop the jumping power of young throwers. This must take place without a load or with a limited additional load. The tasks are modified (height of hurdles, distances between obstacles, etc.) to correspond appropriately to the age and performance range of the young athlete (see Table 3A).

9

TABLE 2: PRINCIPLES OF A METHODICAL USE OF STRENGTH EXERCISES FOR YOUNG (13- TO 14-YEAR-OLD) THROWERS

Weight training exercises (WT): snatch, bench press, press behind the neck, clean and jerk, different pulling exercises in front and behind the body, half knee bends, cleans, ankle exercises, etc.

General strength exercises against the athlete's own body weight (GS): horizontal bar, wall ladder, gymnastic boxes, etc.; push-ups etc.

Gymnastics exercises (GE): trunk exercises with medicine balls, sand bags, partner exercises, exercises using different apparatus (wall ladder, climbing rope, etc.).

Exercise machines.

	Mesocycles			
	1 - 3	4 - 5		6 - 7
Weekly frequency:	2-3x (GE, GS)	2-3x (1x WT, 2x GS)	3-4x (2x WT, 2x GE, GS)	3-4x (2x WT, 2x GE, GS)
Load range:	Explosive performance	30-50%	60-75%	30-50% 60-80%
Number of exercises per training unit	Gymnastics/general strength 8-10 Weight training: 3-5			
Number of reps per series: GE/GS WT	10-15	10-15 12-8	8-10 8-5	8-10 8-5
Total repetitions: GE/GS WT	150-200	150-200 60-120 60-100	75-100 80-120	75-100
Recoveries:	2-4 min	2-4 min		3-5 min

Method: Pyramid system, progressive sets, stations, etc.

GENERAL TRAINING MEANS

General training means include all types of activities—games, gymnastics, skiing, ice skating, swimming, etc.—that involve the basic elements of multifaceted physical and coordinative-technical development. For example, the basic elements of the movement structure could include:

- Combinations of rhythmical running-throwing actions in different movement formats performed in various games.

- Combinations of leg and arm actions performed in various games.

- Development of rhythm in various movement patterns (jumping, rhythm runs, steeplechase, rotational jumps, gymnastics, etc.).

- Striking, slinging and pushing type throws in various games.

- Support, pushoff, stretch and swing elements in gymnastics (tumbling, apparatus).

TABLE 3A: PRINCIPLES OF A METHODICAL USE OF SPRINT AND JUMPING EXERCISES FOR YOUNG THROWERS (13 TO 14 YRS)

Sprinting: starts from different positions, flying start sprints, accelerations, hurdle sprints over low hurdles placed at shorter intervals, sprint ABC (coordination drills with emphasis on frequency).

Jumping: Single- and double-leg takeoffs, horizontal/vertical, bounding, multiple jumps over obstacles (different height boxes, benches, hurdles), depth jumps (low height), high jump, long jump, etc.

	Mesocycles		
	1 - 3	4 - 5	6 - 7
Sprinting emphasis:			
Distances 10-20m	x	xx	xxx
20-30m	xx	xxx	xx
40-80m	xxx	xx	x
50-100m	xx	xx	x
Training unit volume:	0.3-0.5km	0.3-0.5km	0.2-0.3km
Weekly frequency:	2-3	2-3	3-4
Recoveries:	full active recoveries of about 4-8 minutes		
Jumping emphasis:			
Multiple jumps			
5-10	xxx	xx	x
3-5	x	xx	xxx
Single takeoffs			
Horizontal	xx	xx	xx
Vertical	xx	xxx	xx

Method: Double-leg takeoffs dominate. Both sides used in single-leg takeoffs.

Recoveries: 2-3 min between multiple jump series
1-3 min between single jumps

TABLE 3B: PRINCIPLES OF A METHODICAL USE OF GENERAL TRAINING MEANS FOR YOUNG ATHLETES IN MANY-SIDED AND SPECIFIC TRAINING

Training Means	Mesocycles						
	1	2	3	4	5	6	7
General Training (games, gymnastics, swimming, winter sports, etc.)	xx	xxx	xx	xx	xx	x	x
Multifaceted training (sprinting, jumping, general throwing, general strength)	xxx	xx	xxx	xx	xxx	xx	xx
Specific training (specific throwing)	x	x	x	x	xx	xxx	xx

THE YOUNG THROWER

by N. Maltseva, USSR

A short summary of methodical concepts and training guidelines recommended for the development of young throwers, including tests and norms for strength and explosive power indicators for the 11 to 18 years age range.

The continuing improvement of performances in throwing events has forced coaches to pay more attention to the development of the technique and strength of potential future throwers beginning at a very young age. This has been responsible for a variety of methods recommended for the development of young throwing exponents.

It is generally accepted that throwing speed and rhythm change relatively little during the life span of an athlete, but there are virtually no limits to the development of strength capacities. The All-Union Moscow Sport Science Institute therefore recommends the following methodical concepts to develop and improve throwing performances:

1. The employment of lighter implements in the development of throwing techniques.

2. Lighter implements are necessary to establish a "speed-rhythm" structure stereotype. These implements must be used for at least one and a half to two years to develop the performance of fast and precise movement sequence before a change to heavier implements takes place.

3. Heavy implements must not be used during the technique development stage of young athletes .

4. The continually improving strength indicators should remain close to the maximal norms for the corresponding developmental stages, while the rhythm-speed characteristics show relatively little change.

5. Besides the development of general and specific speed capacities, it is important to pay attention to the strength of leg and trunk muscles responsible for a stable vertical posture throughout the throwing movements and the coordination of the support system.

Tables 1 and 2 show the selection and maintenance norms of strength and power indicators in the 11 to 18 years age range applicable to all throwing events.

RECOMMENDED CONCEPTS
Trunk and leg strength (left) and the use of more light implements.

TABLE 1: Strength indicators and norms for 11 to 18 years age range in throwing events.

Exercises	11 yrs	12 yrs	13 yrs	14 yrs	15 yrs	16 yrs	17 yrs	18 yrs
Squat (kg)	—	—	—	70	90	120	160	190
Snatch (kg)	—	—	—	40	60	70	90	100
Clean (kg)	—	—	—	60	80	100	120	145
Dead lift (kg)	—	—	—	—	—	—	180	220

TABLE 2: Power indicators and norms for 11 to 18 yrs age range in throwing events.

Exercises	11 yrs	12 yrs	13 yrs	14 yrs	15 yrs	16 yrs	17 yrs	18 yrs
30m from standing start (sec)	5.00	4.70	4.50	4.30	4.10	4.00	3.90	3.80
Standing long jump (m)	—	—	2.10	2.40	2.60	2.80	2.85	3.00
Standing triple jump (m)	—	6.00	7.00	8.00	8.50	9.00	9.50	10.00
Standing 5 steps (m)	—	10.00	11.00	12.50	13.20	14.00	15.00	16.00
Vertical jump (cm)	—	—	45	60	65	70	75	85
Upward-backward shot throw	—	11.50	13.00	15.00	16.00	15.00	17.00	
Over the head (cm)			(4kg)	(4kg)	(5kg)	(5kg)	(6.26kg)	(6.26kg)

METHODICAL PRINCIPLES

The principles used in the basic teaching stages of throwing events must be understandable to children. The All-Union Moscow Sport Science Institute presented in 1990 a series of principles applicable to events that require a high level of coordination. The following apply to all throwing events:

- The transfer of the bodyweight immediately from the start of the movement from the rear to the front leg. A wide stance assists to perform this task.

- A throwing position in which the left leg and shoulder are leading (for right-handed throwers). This makes it possible to take a sideways position in the preparatory phase of the throw for a wider amplitude in the application of forces.

- Surface contact with both feet throughout the whole throwing movement.

- The throwing movement must be initiated from the ankles and legs.

- The trunk turns forward towards the throwing direction before the arm action begins.

- A sufficiently high delivery angle to increase the throwing distance.

- A rigid left side of the body during the delivery action.

- Because the implement and the hand holding it move at the same velocity, it is important continually to stress arm speed.

TRAINING GUIDELINES

The basic problem in guiding the training of young throwers is to determine the optimal relation between the load volume and the intensity. This applies to the preparation as well as the competition period. Athletes must therefore be allocated an optimal number of maximal intensity (full-effort) throws to be performed in training according to their functional capacities.

A general outline of the distribution of training loads that corresponds with the biological development and the improvement of performances in yearly cycles is presented in Table 3.

TABLE 3: A model of training load distribution over a year for young throwers.

Throwing of training implements	Age in years		
(Number of throws)	13-14	15-16	17-18
Competition implements	1000	1350	1750
Lighter implements	1400	1150	1150
Heavier implements	—	900	1150
Total number throws	2400	3400	4000

Observations and information available from literature make it possible to suggest the following recommendations to guide the training processes of young throwers:

- The intensities of training throws are divided into easy (50% to 80% of the best distance), medium (80 to 90%) and maximal (90 to 100%).

- It is necessary to train with throwing implements three to four times a week during both the preparation and the competition periods.

- The number of throws performed in any one training session must not exceed 25 to 30.

- Training sessions begin with easy throws followed by medium and finally maximal intensity throws.

- The distances of the easy throws should increase parallel to the improvements achieved in the physical performance capacity indicators.

- The total training intensity is determined by the number of throws and their performance effort in any one training session. This applies to the preparation and competition periods.

According to a well-known French author, M. Chabrier, it is important to emphasize general speed and strength development in the early stages of the training of young throwers. This usually leads to rapid and steady improvements in physical performance capacities and throwing distances until the development reaches a plateau.

Training must be reorganized whenever the first signs of stagnation appear. In this case it is advisable to shift emphasis to development of specific speed capacities. This takes place by employing throwing exercises with light implements, performed at maximal speed. Fast strength development exercises are combined with flexibility and mobility training to ensure that the throwing technique amplitude is not restricted.

ORGANIZATION OF BASIC THROWING TRAINING

by Manfred Griesser, Germany

Coaches are faced with several problems in the organization of basic throwing training involving large groups of young athletes. This article looks at the problems and presents a series of practical examples of a methodical approach.

An efficient method of organizing throwing training for young athletes in their initial basic training phase is so-called "group" training. This means an organizational method in which all athletes perform the same tasks together under the direction of the coach. The group method has the following advantages in the development of throwing techniques:

- The athletes can be directed simultaneously under favorable communication conditions.
- The coach has everybody in sight and can observe and correct faulty movements.
- Advice can be called out at any stage during the exercise.

The group training method is particularly suitable for the learning of new movements. It offers favorable possibilities to develop sound "static" positions (delivery position) and the actual delivery movements (standing throws).

ORGANIZATION

In throwing training it is important that the desired action is correctly demonstrated and explained using clear and simple language. In the early stages of learning, where the focus is learning the static positions, it is helpful to make use of ground markings and optical orientation points. Effective group training can only take place when sufficient space is available for all participants. Most suitable for the purpose are hard surfaces that allow the placement of markings on the ground.

The coach in a group training situation has several responsibilities. His initial demonstration must always be extremely correct and easily understandable for the group. All safety measures must be employed (e.g., distance between the athletes, controlled throwing procedures, etc.). Particularly important, naturally, is for the coach to be positioned at an appropriate point. This position must allow clear eye contact with all members of the group and normally should be situated outside the throwing sector on the throwing arm side of the athletes.

PRACTICAL EXAMPLES

1. The Shot Put

Group training is particularly suitable for teaching the delivery position and the standing throw. The following procedures are recommended:

Delivery position:
- Establish the ground markings, indicating the direction line and the position of the feet. An optimal delivery position has about three foot lengths between the two feet (Figure 1).

FIGURE 1: THE OPTIMAL DELIVERY POSITION OF THE FEET IN THE SHOT PUT.

- The athlete takes the delivery position, placing the feet according to the ground markings.

- The body weight is shifted on the right leg, bent so that there is a straight vertical line from the knee to the toes of the right foot (looking from above with a relatively upright position of the upper body).

- The weight is distributed so that the left leg carries no

load. It can be lifted off the surface.

- The left side of the body remains stretched and there is no forward bend in the trunk.

- The eyes are looking back, opposite to the throwing direction. It is advisable to use an orientation point.

- The virtually straight left arm is directed opposite to the throwing direction.

Standing put:
- The coach explains how the shot should be held in the hand.

- The shot is placed close to the forward part of the neck with the elbow nearly under the shot. A position where the shot is pressed with a high elbow against the back of the neck, as observed in many top-class athletes, is not recommended for young athletes.

- The athlete settles in the standing put position.

- The delivery is a stretching movement in a sequence of foot, knee and hip joint.

- The athlete aims to remain "tall" during the delivery with both feet in contact with the surface (no reverse).

- The use of orientation points for the delivery stretch and the release angle of the shot are recommended.

Medicine balls can be used indoors for the development of the standing put. In this situation it is important to observe that the difficulty in holding a medicine ball in one hand does not lead to an incorrect performance of the standing put. In order to settle in the correct position it is necessary for the left hand to support the ball. The left lower arm should here be placed in a position that corresponds approximately to the delivery angle. All other aspects of the medicine ball put follow the above described procedures.

2. The Ball Throw

The first throwing event the young athletes learn is the ball throw. The learning processes of this event can occur faster when the group method is employed and all athletes perform the single stages together.

After the young athletes have become familiar with the standing ball throw (using a bent or straight arm), it is advisable to proceed as soon as possible to the learning of the impulse stride. The following procedures are recommended:

1. The establishment of the initial position:

   - stride position with the left leg forward,

   - throwing arm straight,

- body weight slightly on the right leg.

2. The performance of the impulse stride without delivery:

   - marking of the impulse stride on the surface (Figure 2), including the positioning of the feet (the right foot deviation of about 45° sideways after the impulse stride),

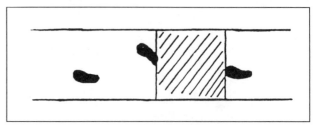

**FIGURE 2: MAKING OF THE IMPULSE STRIDE
IN THE JAVELIN THROW.**

   - performance of a flat impulse stride over the marked lines with a slight backward lean of the upper body, a straight throwing arm,

   - and a fast, heel first, placement of the support leg.

3. The performance of the impulse stride with delivery:

   - the delivery is initiated from a forward-upward drive of the support leg,

   - the arm moves over the head during the delivery (not sideways!).

4. Recommendations for a three-stride rhythm:

   - a basic initial position with a straight throwing arm,

   - the first stride taken with the left leg (for right-handed throwers),

   - the impulse stride, followed by the delivery position.

It is important to establish a precise runup in the learning of the total ball throw. The athlete must reach exactly the clearly marked checkpoint of the impulse stride box in order to concentrate for the transfer from the run to the impulse stride. Right-handed throwers hit the check mark with the left foot. The following basic points are observed in the total throw:

- a stable throwing position,

- a slight backward lean of the body,

- a straight throwing arm.

3. The Javelin Throw

The leg work developed in the ball throw is carried over to the initial learning stage of the javelin throw. The first technical tasks are therefore the establishment of the standing throw, the impulse stride and the three-stride rhythm. This is followed by the learning of a five-stride rhythm:

- The initial position features the right leg forward, the javelin held relaxed at about head height.

- The preliminary stride is taken with the left leg, including at the same time a slight forward movement of the throwing arm and shoulder.

- The second and third walking strides are made with an active straight-line withdrawal of the javelin until the throwing arm is stretched.

- The combination of the javelin withdrawal with the impulse stride and the planting of the support leg (fifth stride).

- The five-stride rhythm should be performed first without the delivery and finally with the full throwing action.

- It is important to observe that the throwing arm remains stretched during the impulse stride.

As the actions of the runup are learned they should be performed within the total throw in progressive stages, first walking, then jogging, and finally with a relaxed acceleration run. The precision of the runup is again important as the athlete must hit the check mark indicating the start of the five-stride rhythm.

4. The Discus Throw

There is a remarkable similarity between the throwing positions of the shot put and the discus throw (i.e., the positions of the feet, legs, body and joint angles). This makes it possible to use all the exercise variations employed in the development procedures of the shot put.

Safety precautions are extremely important in the discus throw, and the recommended formations for group

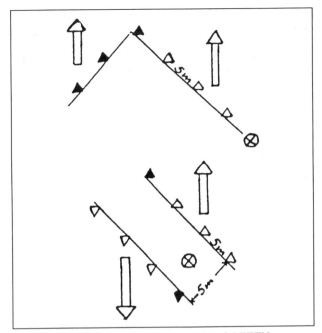

FIGURE 3: RECOMMENDED SAFETY PRECAUTIONS.

training are shown in Figure 3. Group training should not take place in locations where a lack of space prevents adherence to the required safety measures.

Standing Throw:

- The standing throw begins with relaxed preliminary swings of the throwing arm in the direction of the left foot.

- The delivery movement is initiated from a rotational drive of the right side of the body (foot, knee and hip joints).

- The discus leaves the hand at the height of the throwing arm shoulder or slightly lower.

- The top of the hand points upward during the release, and the discus leaves the hand in a flat flight.

- Both feet must remain in contact with the surface after the delivery (no reverse).

RELEASE VELOCITY—THE MAIN AIM IN THROWING EVENTS

by Winfried Joch, Germany

A summary of selected major technique, conditioning and talent development factors presented at the International Seminar for Javelin and Hammer Throws, held in Berlin in 1987.

The extended International Seminar for Javelin and Hammer Throws staged in the Eastern half of the then still divided city of Berlin covered the performance development of the two events, structural assumptions, analyses of performances, and the necessary strength training for athletes contesting these events from beginners to high-performance exponents. The aim of the seminar was to provide a forum for an exchange of experiences between the 80 participants from 26 countries.

The results and the "reliable" knowledge shared at the seminar brought to light an abundance of detailed information and, moreover, highlighted five major points:

- Improvement of performances has not come to an end. For the hammer throw, 90 meters may be looked at as a short-term aim. Although the new javelin has made the situation in the men's event uncertain, a 90-meter target represents here a realistic target, while the women are aiming to reach 80 meters. [Editor's note: this has already been achieved.]

- The most important parameter in achieving these goals is the improvement of release velocity to 32m/sec. for men and 26m/sec. for women.

- To reach such targets requires a further increase of the quality, volume and intensity of training. All three of these areas should be considered equally.

- There are at present, even within individual countries, very different training systems in existence. This means that, besides the generally accepted and scientifically approved approaches, there are peculiar, individual systems. This applies, in particular to the high-performance range, where a large spectrum of training variations is evident.

- The road to high-level performances leads initially through the first step of "talent identification training," as talent is in reality revealed only in training.

Without going into critical examination or elaboration, it appears that the following selected details from the seminar addresses are particularly significant:

1. A premature development of any physical capacity—particularly maximal strength—limits the development of talented potential. Technical faults have proved to restrict performance.

This statement should make it clear that technique training must be in the foreground during the development of beginners. Only when the technical level has reached a certain stability can the improvement of performance take place through the development of maximal strength values.

A reversed approach leads through faulty technique to injury and a disproportional relationship between the contributions of optimal movement structure and strength to the technique achieved. A "refined" mastery of technique should be achieved within two or three years of starting basic training.

All training loads have to be systematically applied in order to avoid injury. It should be kept in mind here that strength development in the training of beginners (12- to 18-year-old athletes) has no significant importance, as it will be virtually impossible later to make up for any shortcomings in technique and coordination. Nevertheless, it is important that some cohesion exists between "technique" and "conditioning."

A certain level of strength is indispensable for optimal execution of movement; however, in the training of beginners it serves only to assist improvement of technique and movement structure. Strength at this stage is not employed to maximize performance.

Ruth Fuchs

2.   From a mechanical viewpoint, the distance of a throw depends on the velocity of the release, the angle of the release and the height of the release. The velocity of the release is, in practice, the most important of these factors. It is in this parameter that the reserves for better performance are hidden.

The release velocity on the East German hammer throw record (82.64m) was 29.3m/sec., the angle of release 38°. A larger angle of release, according to the opinions of experts, would have had a negative influence on the release velocity. This has to be improved to about 32m/sec. in order to reach a distance close to 90m. It shows the importance of the velocity. Athletes have to be taught to be in the position to exploit a higher level of muscular strength in a shorter time. Obviously, the time component is a performance-reducing factor.

The development of speed plays a decisive role in the level of performance, above all in the training of beginners. They should start the development of technique with a 2kg(!) hammer, with the weight of the implement being thereafter increased step by step. At age 17 a beginner should be capable of reaching a target distance of over 80m with a hammer of light weight. The temporal-dynamic structure of the throw should at this stage be close to the final high-performance model.

The increase of the hammer weight presents a secondary training and competition target. The use of lightweight hammers is therefore not only a significant training method but also provides an effective competitive impetus during basic training. The attainment of the maximal possible release velocity is the aim in all the single stages of development.

3.   The whole training program of beginners is carefully planned and based on reaching set standard values in each development stage. Admittedly, the multi-faceted approach to training should not be overlooked. Besides their specific training, even hammer throwers take part in games and are involved in intensive gymnastics programs. They hurdle, sprint and jump and, in addition, participate in a specific program to develop coordinative capacities.

Hammer training should be rich in variation and based on systematic changes in the training load. The variety of exercises becomes narrower and more specific only in the high-performance range. The reason for this multi-faceted approach is explained by:

- The need, above all, to develop and establish perfect muscular balance, because in the framework of whole body movements (this applies to all track & field events) the total system is only as strong as its weakest link.

- The requirement of a large number of exercises and stimuli for an optimal stimulation of the central nervous system, which is responsible for the control of movements and for inter- and intramuscular coordination.

4.   The noteworthy contribution by Prof. M. Buhrle (Freiburg) established a scientific background for strength training and was presented in a practically oriented format. Buhrle's address was based on research results obtained at the University of Freiburg and included information from Buhrle's and Schmidtbleicher's publications on the development of maximal strength and power. Three aspects stood out in the 90-minute address:

- Maximal strength is, like explosive strength, a basic quality of power. This reveals clearly that maximal strength and power have no counteracting influence on each other. A high level of maximal strength has therefore no negative influence on power.

- The improvement of maximal strength occurs in two different ways—through an increase of the cross-section of the muscle and through an arbitrary activation of the largest possible number of muscle fibers.

Different training methods are employed for these two purposes. The increase of the cross-section of the muscle is effected by using a large number of repetitions in strength training. Twelve repetitions, in which the last one is just achievable, can here be regarded as a guideline. The load is between 75 and 85% of the maximum and the work continues until exhaustion.

The improvement of activating potential takes place by

TABLE 1: NORM VALUES FOR JAVELIN TALENT (12/13 YEARS).

Test	Boys	Girls
Ball throw* (12 years)	65-70m	55-60m
(13 years)	70-75m	60-65m
60m from standing start (sec.)	8.30	8.50
30m from flying start (sec.)	4.25	4.00
Triple hop (m)	6.50	6.50
800m run (min.)	2.25	2.35

* = The weight of the ball is not stated. Normally the balls used in the GDR weighed 150g.

using short maximal loads (one to three repetitions) against extremely high resistances (95 to 100%). The work occurs in a relatively fatigue-free condition with long recoveries and explosive efforts.

- Large numbers of sets and repetitions have a deteriorating effect on the arbitrary activation potential of muscle fibers. This means that there is considerable difference between the "theoretically" possible contraction performance of a muscle and the actual contraction effected ("strength deficit"). On the other hand, strength training based on the "short maximal contrac-

tion" method influences an optimal utilization of the cross-section of a muscle.

5. "Talent identification training" in the German Democratic Republic was based on a "guide values" system, representing information points used at the start of basic training (see Table 1), as well as during the various developmental stages of an athlete's career (Table 2—Hammer Throw, Table 3—Javelin Throw). It is here noticeable that:

- The choice of test exercises is relatively limited and identical.

- A considerable range of variation is acceptable as "norm" performances (for example, the snatch in Table 3).

6. Finally, another noteworthy statement:

Basic scientific knowledge is an important factor in coaching. Admittedly, it must be combined with the practical experience of the coach, as the guidance of training can never depend solely on scientific data. It simply doesn't work without experimentation and without taking into consideration the individual peculiarities of an athlete. The experimentation, however, should take place within parameters established using scientifically validated basic data.

TABLE 2: DEVELOPMENT DATA OF GUNTHER RODEHAU (GDR HAMMER RECORD SETTER, 82.64M, IN 1985).

Competition performance (m)	70	80	82.40
8kg hammer (m)	61.00	74.00	76.40
6kg hammer (m)	76.00	85.00	87.70
30m from flying start (sec.)	3.15	3.10	3.11
St. triple jump (m)	9.50	10.50	—
St. long jump (m)	—	—	3.38
Snatch (kg)	115	145	—
Squat (kg)	230	290	310
Clean (kg)	150	170	—

TABLE 3: DEVELOPMENT DATA OF RUTH FUCHS (GDR JAVELIN RECORD SETTER, 69.96M, IN 1980) AND PETRA FELKE (GDR JAVELIN RECORD SETTER, 75.40M, IN 1985).

	FUCHS			FELKE		
Age (Yrs.)	23	25	33	18	22	26
Year	1970	1972	1980	1977	1981	1985
Performance (m)	60.60	65.06	69.96	61.24	66.60	75.40
800g javelin (m)	48.24	53.20	59.32	—	50.50	59.00
Snatch (kg)	65.0	77.5	92.5	42.5	70.0	100.0
30m flying (sec.)	3.67	3.28	3.29	—	—	—
Triple hop (m)	8.22	8.80	9.35	—	—	—
4kg shot backwards (m)	14.46	16.00	19.30	12.80	—	—

STRENGTH TRAINING PRINCIPLES

by Merv Kemp, Australia

A summary of what is involved in contemporary strength development, covering the principles and different methods employed to improve strength and power capacities.

PRINCIPLES

Before looking at the details of working out a training program there are several points that must be understood.

PROGRESSIVE LOAD INCREASE

Strength increases will occur only if the neuromuscular system is subjected to ever increasing levels of stress. This can be achieved by increasing the load, the number of sets, and the number of repetitions, as well as by reducing the rest interval between sets.

For novice athletes increases in strength can occur in a linear fashion, but for advanced athletes the stress load should increase over time in an undulatory manner. This is illustrated in Figure 1. After two weeks of heavy training an unloading phase should follow, during which the work volume is greatly reduced to allow for supercompensation.

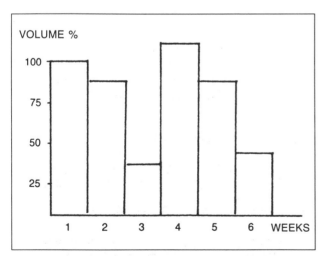

FIGURE 1: LOAD INCREASES IN STRENGTH TRAINING. FOR ADVANCED ATHLETES THE LOAD IS INCREASED IN AN UNDULATORY MANNER

VARIETY

It is important to change the nature of the training program frequently because the neuromuscular system rapidly adjusts to the training regimen. Variety can be achieved in several ways:

- Load magnitude: extensive, intensive, submaximal, maximal and supramaximal.

- Method of contraction: isometric, concentric, eccentric.

- Speed of contraction. Varying contraction speed results in faster strength gains. Lifting slowly eliminates the assistance of momentum, and thereby creates greater tension in the muscles and facilitates hypertrophy. Neural stimulation is high when high-speed movements are used.

- Changing the exercise. Leg strength, for example, can be developed by back squats, step-ups, front squats, leg press, back squats, leg extensions and hamstring curls.

To achieve the desired training effect on the muscular system it is important that the training undertaken is appropriate to the desired outcome. For example, a training program consisting of three sets of 20 repetitions will not develop speed strength.

For an exercise to be effective it must transfer to the competition movement. Strong triceps are important in the shot put and can be developed by dips, for example. But, as an exercise, dips have less effective transfer than incline bench press, which also develops the triceps.

MAXIMAL CONTRACTION METHODS

The following methods will aid the development of maximum strength by stimulating the neuromuscular system. These methods will increase strength without any great increase in body weight or hypertrophy. Such methods are very intensive.

Narrow pyramid approach

This method involves near-maximal concentric contractions

90%	95%	97%	100%	95%	90%
3	2	1	1	2	3

Note: A thorough warmup should be undertaken at lesser percentages of the one-repetition maximum (ORM, i.e., the heaviest weight at which one repetition can be performed). Rest intervals of 3-5 minutes should be taken between sets.

Maximal concentric contractions

Bulgarian weightlifters use this method, and only experienced athletes should attempt it. The method consists of five sets of one repetition at 100% with rest intervals of 3-5 minutes between sets.

Maximal isometric contractions

Five sets of two repetitions held for 5-6 seconds with three-minute rest intervals. **Note:** This type of exercise does not promote intermuscular coordination. Its main use is in rehabilitation from injury.

Maximal eccentric contractions

Loads up to 150% of the ORM for a concentric contraction are used. For women, loads should be restricted to about 110-120% of the ORM. Perform three sets of five repetitions with three-minute rest intervals. **Note:** Unless special equipment is available, training partners (spotters) are essential.

Eccentric-concentric contractions

This approach employs different types of muscular contraction within a session, within a series or within a single repetition. It combines the benefits of eccentric contractions against supramaximal loads with the intermuscular coordination of concentric contractions. Two alternative approaches are as follows:

- Using a load of 70-90%, lower the barbell over a period of 6-8 seconds then raise as quickly as possible. Up to five sets of 6-8 repetitions are recommended with 4-5 minute rest intervals.

- Load the barbell to 120% of the ORM for concentric contraction and lower over 4-6 seconds. When the barbell reaches the bottom of its movement, training partners remove 40% of the load and the barbell is raised as quickly as possible. Recommended are 3-4 sets of 1-2 repetitions with 4-5 minute rest intervals.

Another way of combining different types of muscular contractions is the so called static-dynamic method. This approach is possible in two exercises—squat and bench press. After the lowering eccentric movement, the concentric contraction, working against gravity, is halted halfway through and the barbell is held stationary (isometric action) for a few seconds before completing the lift as explosively as possible. When the load is 60-80% each pause should be 1-2 seconds; 4-6 reps are recommended. For loads over 85%, the pause should be 2-3 seconds with repetitions numbering between two and four.

SUB-MAXIMAL CONTRACTION METHODS

These methods can promote hypertrophy and an increase in body weight. Modifications of these methods can enhance speed strength or strength endurance.

Loads from 60-80% are used with a high number of sets and repetitions, making such methods extensive in their nature.

Muscular exhaustion results from the exertion of force at speeds ranging from slow to fast. By performing repetitions to exhaustion, maximum tension is produced within the muscle. It should be noted that synchronized firing of nerve impulses in the muscle fiber is maximized only in the last couple of repetitions, so it is important that the load and repetitions be sufficient to exhaust the muscle.

Constant load

Suitable for promoting hypertrophy. The load remains constant and the number of repetitions and sets is fairly high.

For young athletes

50% x 5 sets	or	60% x 5 sets
12 reps		8-10 reps

For advanced athletes

80% x 5 reps
8-10 reps

Rest pauses should be of 3-4 minutes duration.

These routines aim at working the musculature to exhaustion. Training partners may be required to complete the last few repetitions.

Progressively increasing load

70%	80%	85%	90%	95%
12	10	7	3	2

Rest pauses should be of 4-5 minutes duration.

As the number of repetitions is high, some assistance from a training partner may be needed in order to complete the last reps in a set.

Routines such as those described above develop intermuscular and intramuscular coordination and can be supplemented in the following ways:

- **Super Sets**—Two different exercises are performed without any rest between sets. For example, a set of curls (working the biceps, the agonist) is followed immediately with a set of dips (which work the triceps, the antagonist).

- **Negative repetitions (eccentric)**—After a set of dynamic contractions perform 2-3 eccentric reps with an additional 25% load.

- **Cheated repetitions**—After exhausting the muscle group extra reps are attempted by employing other muscle groups in an incorrect movement—e.g., performing curls while swinging the torso forward and back. Be careful to avoid injury.

- **Pre-exhaustion**—A muscle group is worked in isolation and then is immediately involved in a compound movement with other muscle groups. For example, the hamstrings can be worked on a machine then worked again together with other muscles in a set of squats.

OTHER METHODS

Isokinetics

A device on an isokinetic machine adjusts the effective load throughout the range of movement so that the muscle contracts at a constant speed. The Kin-Com machine used by physical therapists provides for eccentric and concentric contractions and is useful in developing hypertrophy and absolute strength.

It should be noted that isokinetic machines do not allow for the motor acceleration variations which occur in sprints, jumps and throws. Consequently such machines could train the muscle in ways inappropriate for dynamic events. Isokinetics can be useful in the early stages of the preparation phase.

Isometrics

It seems a paradox that, despite the static nature of isometric exercises, there is a high correlation between isometric maximal strength and movement speed. Increases in movement speed result from increases in isometric strength.

Soviet strength experts draw a distinction between "pure isometric strength" and "functional isometric strength." In the former the muscles contract against a fixed resistance, but in the latter a weight is first lifted then pushed or pulled against an immovable resistance.

Isometric contraction is a supplementary training method for the development of maximum strength. It has been recommended that isometric work should comprise 10% of the total workload with concentric and eccentric work representing 70% and 20% respectively. Isometrics can be valuable for rehabilitation purposes. Three to five sets of maximal contractions held for 10-12 seconds with three-minute rest intervals between sets are recommended.

Combined

These methods can develop hypertrophy and inter- and intramuscular coordination.

- A combined method with the emphasis on incurring hypertrophy can be described as a wide pyramid:

60%	65%	70%	75%	80%	75%	70%	65%	60%
8	7	6	5	4	5	6	7	8

or

60% x 2	65% x 2	70% x 2	75% x 2	80% x 2
8	7	6	5	4

- The following approach—a combined method emphasizing coordination—is referred to as a repeated pyramid.

70% x 2	80% x 2	85% x 2	90% x 2	95% x 2
5	4	3	2	1

REACTIVE METHODS

- **Hopping**—On both legs: (a) at one's own rhythm or (b) for maximum number of ground contacts or for (c) maximum height. Three sets of 30 reps with five-minute rest intervals. For advanced athletes, single leg hopping is recommended in 3 sets of 10 reps with four- to five-minute rest intervals.

- **Jumping/Bounding**—Alternate hopping and stepping—three sets of 20 reps with five-minute rest intervals. Standing triple jumps, 3-5 jumps, five sets of 8-10 reps with five-minute rest intervals. Jumping over hurdles set about 1m apart, with height and number to depend upon age and ability.

  Hopping over a distance of 25m as fast as possible—five sets of 3-5 reps with five-minute rest intervals between reps and 10-minute rest intervals between sets. **Note:** These drills are very suitable for testing the athlete's physical condition.

- **Depth Jumps**—An action of jumping down from a height of up to 80cm, then following immediately with a jump forward for distance or a jump up for height. Perform three to five sets of 10 reps with 10-minute rest intervals. **Note:** If the athlete's heels touch the ground the height is excessive. If the contact time with the ground is too long the exercise has little benefit, so avoid jumping onto soft surfaces, except for the final landing. Depth jumps are suitable only for well-conditioned athletes. The use of additional loads such as weighted jackets is not advised for orthopedic reasons and because additional loading causes rapid fatigue.

Reactive training methods stimulate the neuromuscular system and are performed best when the athlete is well rested. Such training methods help to convert the generalized strength developed with barbells into functional strength as required in the competition movement. Some throwers sadly neglect this aspect of their training and become obsessed with the development of general strength. Being able to squat a huge weight like 300kg is of little value if the athlete can only manage a standing long jump of 2.30m.

DEVELOPMENT PRINCIPLES

Speed Strength

It has already been stated that speed strength is developed with an increase in maximum strength. But speed strength can also be improved without an increase in maximum strength by the following methods:

- With barbells, $\frac{35\text{-}50\% \times 5}{7}$ performed fast with 3-4 minutes rest intervals. The weight is accelerated in the concentric phase only.

- Throwing lightweight implements.

- Reduced resistance training—downhill running.

- Plyometrics—reactive training.

These methods should be performed at nearly maximum intensity and the athlete needs to be fresh. Terminate the activity with the onset of fatigue.

Strength Endurance

Strength endurance involves work against resistances exceeding 30% of the individual's maximum strength. Methods used should relate to the strength requirements of the event and the time taken for the event.

Short term endurance is increased with an increase in maximum strength. Medium term endurance may be improved by employing:

1. $\underline{40\text{-}60\% \times 3\text{-}5 \text{ sets}}$; rest intervals 1-1$\frac{1}{2}$ minutes.
   10-20 reps

2. Circuit training, 6-12 stations, 40 seconds of work at each with a 20- to 40-second rest interval. Perform 2-6 sets of the circuit,

Long term endurance may be increased as follows:

$$\underline{30\text{-}40\% \times 4\text{-}6 \text{ sets,}}$$
$$30 \text{ reps}$$

with rest intervals of 1-1$\frac{1}{2}$ minutes.

Specific Strength

To transfer general strength to the competition movement special exercises are used. Specific strength is developed through exercises which in part involve an element of the competition movement—for example, incline bench press for the shot put. Special strength involves the full competition movement performed with an additional resistance. Examples include throwing an 8kg hammer or running up a slight incline.

Specific strength can be developed in four ways:

1. Imitative exercises which reflect technical aspects of the competition movement; e.g.:

   - imitating the delivery action in the discus with a 5kg plate,

   - holding light dumbbells in the hand and imitating the arm action of a sprinter.

2. General strength exercises performed with the speed, rhythm or intensity of the competition event. For throwers and jumpers, Olympic lifts performed at near maximal intensity are examples. Sprinters could perform as many squats as possible in 10 seconds with a load of 60%.

3. Exercises that focus on the muscle groups primarily involved in the competition movement. Care should be taken to ensure that the different body segments follow paths similar to those they follow in the technical movement. For example, a high jumper could perform step-ups with a barbell resting on the shoulders and simultaneously swing the free leg in a manner imitating the takeoff action.

4. Exercises in which the muscular tension is similar to that generated while performing the competition movement, as in the case of depth jumps for jumpers.

Specific strength exercises aim at a qualitative improvement of the muscles used in the competition movement. However, these exercises must reflect the temporal and spatial characteristics of that movement. This is known as dynamic accord.

REFERENCES

1. Hancock, T. *Practical Aspects of Resistance Training.*
2. Schmidtbleicher, D. *Strength and Strength Training.* First Elite Coaches Conference, Canberra, Australia, 1985.
3. Pedemonte, J. *Notes from Australian Lecture Tour,* 1986.
4. Matveyev, L. *Fundamentals of Sport Training.* Progress Publishers, Moscow, USSR.
5. Pyke, F.S. (ed). *Towards Better Coaching.* Australian Government Publishing Services, Canberra.
6. Schmolinsky, G. *Track and Field.* Sportverlag Berlin, German Democratic Republic.
7. Dick, F; Johson, C; Paish, W. *Strength Training for Athletics.* British Amateur Athletic Board, London, England.

STRENGTH TRAINING— EQUIPMENT CONSIDERATIONS

by Dr. Bill Tancred, Great Britain

The author, a former elite discus thrower, describes the various types of devices available for emphasizing different types of muscle contractions in strength development.

There are many methods and modes of resistance against which muscles are systematically worked in strength training—including iron weights, hydraulic pressure, elastic tubing, compressed air, steel springs, water and electrical resistance. Maximizing the forces produced by contracting muscles is the goal of this form of athletics conditioning.

The Principle of Progressive Resistance is basic to strength development. The principle holds that if someone wants to get stronger, exercise must be performed against gradually increasing resistance. Nearly all strength training equipment is designed to provide progressive resistance for various muscle groups.

As different sorts of strength training equipment emphasize different types of muscle contractions, it is important to understand the characteristics of positive, negative and static contractions.

Positive contractions occur during the "lifting" phase of an exercise. To lift, the involved muscles must generate a contractile force that exceeds the resistance provided. Once the required force is achieved, the muscle fibers shorten and move the joints they control.

Negative contractions take place when a resistance is "lowered" or returned to a starting position. The involved muscles continue to generate a contractile force, but it is less than the force provided by the resistance. The muscle fibers lengthen and body segments return to their original position.

Static contractions take place when muscle fibers develop tension. There is no change in the length of the fibers, however. The contractile force is equal to the resistive force. During static contractions, there is no movement of the joints which the involved muscles activate.

The strength of positive and negative contractions tends to vary with the speed of movement. This happens because of internal muscular friction, and it can be of consequence during strength training.

For example, if you can slowly lift (positive contraction) 100 kilograms, then you can slowly lower (negative contraction) about 140 kilograms. Interestingly, you can hold motionless (static contraction) approximately 120 kilograms, midway between your positive and negative strength levels.

VARIOUS TYPES OF STRENGTH-TRAINING EQUIPMENT

How do these facts relate to strength training equipment? Perhaps the most basic strength training tools are free weights. Barbells and dumbbells provide a fixed resistance that requires varying amounts of muscle force for positive, negative and static contractions.

Because positive strength is less than negative and static strength, the lifting phase of free-weight exercises requires more effort than the other phases. Nonetheless, all three types of muscle contractions are effectively incorporated into free-weight training, especially at slow movement speeds.

Weight-Stack Machines

Strength training machines utilizing weight stacks function similarly to free-weight training because they also involve positive, negative and static contractions.

Static Devices

Static strength training devices do not permit positive or negative muscle contractions and appear to be position-specific. That is, the muscles develop more strength at the trained position than at other positions in their movement range. Because this type of exercise often elicits excessive rises in blood pressure, it generally is not recommended for adult strength training participants.

Isokinetic Equipment

Many machines—including some that use hydraulic pressure, friction clutches and electrical resistance—are limited to positive movements. They offer resistance only when the athlete is performing positive muscle contractions. The resistance drops to zero once the positive movement is stopped.

Some of the machines in this category are known as isokinetic training devices and can be set for specific movement speeds (e.g., 60°/second, 120°/second, and so on). The machine resistance increases in direct proportion to the applied muscle force, but the speed of movement remains constant.

Although isokinetic strength training can produce less muscle soreness, it does not permit negative or static muscle contractions.

There is currently no commercial strength equipment that provides negative-only training. However, certain machines now are designed to emphasize negative muscle contractions by automatically increasing resistance during the negative phase of exercise. Because of greater resistance required for high-effort negative contractions, this type of training may carry with it an increased risk of injury.

Conversely, free weights and weight-stack machines provide a significant negative component during the lowering movements. If one performs the positive contraction first, the potential for injury is greatly reduced. This is true especially when lowering is performed in a slow, controlled manner.

It is worth bearing in mind that in free-weight and weight-stack exercises the resistance force determines muscle force, but in isokinetic exercises, muscle force determines the resistive force.

MATCHING RESISTANCE AND MUSCLE STRENGTH

An additional aspect of strength training is the matching of exercise resistance to muscle strength potential throughout the range of movement.

The muscles and bones serve as lever systems that have mechanical disadvantages in other positions. Consequently, the effective force of contraction varies considerably from point to point.

Some equipment manufacturers have attempted to vary the exercise resistance in accordance with the effective muscle strength. Their machines provide less resistance in weaker joint positions and more resistance in stronger joint positions.

For example, when performing a bench press, the applied muscle force increases greatly as the arms extend. This is because of more favorable leverage arrangements.

Nautilus-type machines use an oval cam and chain arrangement to change the force applied to the resistance throughout the range of movement. Some Universal Gym-type equipment incorporates a lever arm with a moving fulcrum to accomplish the same purpose.

By design, isokinetic strength training matches the machine resistance to the muscular effort. Because isokinetic equipment is set for a specific movement speed, an increase in applied muscle force produces a corresponding increase in resistance. But as mentioned previously, this relationship exists only for positive muscle contractions.

SEPARATE MUSCLE TRAINING

One of the concepts long associated with successful strength training is muscle isolation. A particular muscle group can usually be worked harder when it is trained individually rather than in conjunction with other muscle groups.

Most people, for example, think of the bench press as a chest exercise. Although the chest muscles play a major role, the front shoulder muscles, triceps muscles, and forearm muscles are essential to performance of this exercise.

These muscles are smaller and weaker than the chest muscles, and fatigue quickly. As a result, the exercise is often terminated before the chest muscles have been worked fully.

Apply Resistance Directly

Some equipment manufacturers have addressed this problem by developing separate machines for each major muscle group. Rather than incorporate the hands and arms, the resistance is applied directly to the attachment area of the target muscle group.

For example, because the chest muscles attach to the upper arms, resistance pads are positioned against the upper arms. In this manner, many of the weaker muscles of the hands and arms are eliminated and the exercise can be continued until the chest muscles are thoroughly fatigued.

Rotary Movement for Muscle Isolation

Although it is not possible to isolate individual muscle groups completely, direct resistance is a first step. A second step is to provide rotary movement in each exercise.

Rotary movements, such as knee extensions, involve a single joint action which limits the number of contributing muscle groups. Conversely, movements such as bench presses involve two or more joints and several major muscle groups.

Many strength machines are designed specifically to provide resistance through a full range of rotary movement, enhancing muscle isolation.

ACHIEVING STRENGTH SAFELY

Exercise safety should be the highest priority for all strength training enthusiasts. If an exercise or exercise device is potentially dangerous, it should be eliminated. There is nothing worse than incurring an injury because of one's sincere effort to attain better fitness.

Use Help in Training

Certain barbell exercises, such as bench presses, incline presses, and squats, for instance, should always be performed with the assistance of a spotter. By doing so one may avoid the obvious danger of being trapped under a heavy weight and, additionally, it is important to have help taking the barbell from the supports and returning it there.

The need for help also exists with many exercise machines. Assistance may be necessary to avoid overstretching or overloading the muscles when getting in and out of the apparatus.

Durable and Safe Equipment

The supportive structure of most strength training machines is itself a significant safety feature. Many strength training machines now are designed to prevent contact with moving parts. Likewise, the high quality materials and precision components used by prominent equipment companies greatly reduce the risk of accidents.

During the past several years, market forces have pushed manufacturers to produce equipment that is competitively well constructed and durable. Nonetheless, all equipment will wear better with proper care and cleaning. I am a strong advocate of preventative maintenance and daily servicing to ensure that equipment is functional and smooth-running.

MOTIVATION IS THE KEY

Motivation is vitally important for most men, women and youth beginning a strength training program.

While every type of exercise equipment is novel and exciting during the first few weeks of training, motivation is the key to continued participation and improved fitness.

Sometimes simple forms of reinforcement, such as seeing more weight on your barbells or weight stacks, are the most motivating.

Choose Equipment and Facilities Wisely

As a coach, fitness club owner or instructor, put yourself in the place of your team or club members. Make the effort to visit various training facilities and try their equipment.

Carefully observe the equipment construction, movement mechanics and wear patterns. Note the functional components, performance feedback, the feel of each exercise. If, after careful experimentation, you are highly satisfied with the equipment, your athletes probably will be equally pleased.

I recommend that the purchase of new strength training equipment be predicated on actual experience. Brochures and showrooms are always enticing, but the best way to select equipment wisely is by using it in training.

TRAINING OF TECHNIQUE AND SPECIFIC POWER IN THROWING EVENTS

by Dr. Klaus E. Bartonietz, Germany

Dr. Bartonietz, a biomechanist and training advisor at the Rhineland Olympic Training Center, Germany, presents some biomechanical findings and their practical application in throwing events, including the problems with the use of heavy implements.

The technique of the competition movements is for all track & field events the most important base of the performance. Technique determines the effectiveness of the interaction between all factors, influencing the result. Technique and abilities are the two sides of one complex phenomenon: the athlete's movement. The technique, therefore, is developing continuously with the growing abilities. Conversely, growing abilities demand changes in technique.

1. MORE POWER FOR A GREATER RANGE

To reach a greater distance the athlete must be able to realize a higher power level for acceleration (P_a) in order to transplant more kinetic energy (ΔE_{kin}) in a shorter time interval (Δt) to the segments of the body and to the implement:

$$Pa = \frac{\Delta E_{kin}}{\Delta t} \quad (W)$$

The kinetic energy increases because the velocity of the release must be faster. More intensive acceleration and deceleration movements of body parts are the pre-condition for higher muscular pre-tension during the delivery. With improving performance, the time for the movement shortens as the result of a higher velocity level. It should be noted here that the athlete must also perform work to lift the implement and therefore also produce the power to lift the implement in the vertical direction.

A greater power level requires the ability to perform more work as immediately as possible under event-specific conditions. Athletes achieve this by using heavy weights and specific strength exercises. The available power

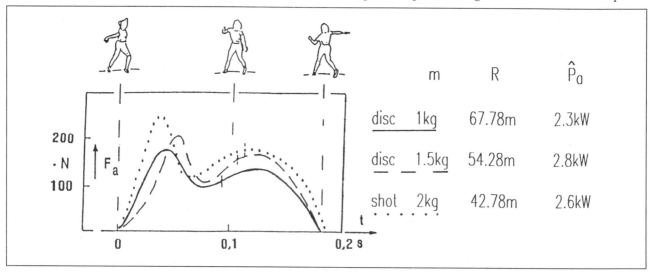

FIGURE 1: FORCE-TIME RELATION AND POWER DATA OF A DISCUS THROWER USING DIFFERENT WEIGHT IMPLEMENTS

is the key problem of training, because skills and abilities are expressed together in power.

In the end, problems with performance in different movement conditions (throws from the stand, short runup, light and heavy implements) in relation to the competition movement or in using different techniques, can be explained by the available power level. That will be shown with the help of the following examples.

Exercises with greater power demands are the effective way to develop special power abilities. Heavier implements challenge greater power values and contribute to developing a greater power level than the competition exercise. Figure 1 illustrates the higher power demands of heavy implements for a discus thrower.

The same principle applies to other events—top male shot putters reach a higher power level with the 8kg implement than with the 7.26kg shot as do female athletes with the 5kg shot (Bartonietz 1987, 1992).

The data in Figure 1 shows the highest power demands and how the effectiveness of very heavy implements depends on the level of performance. Just because Baryishnikov *could* use a 10kg shot (Palm 1990), the employment of such an implement is not indicated to be generally effective for a top athlete.

We must here take into consideration substantial unbeneficial changes in the movement pattern (specifically, the development of an emphasis on upper body work and poor conditions for the left leg work). Palm's conclusion that the right leg activity is the decisive element (analyzing Baryishnikov) must be corrected. The right leg has a triggering function, as the decisive element during the delivery is the bracing left leg. This is valid not only for the rotational technique but also for the glide.

A greater application of power to the implement is the result of greater power available from the leg and trunk work, creating a higher pre-tension of the muscle groups for the final arm movement (javelin, shot or discus) or for the impetus during the double-support phases (hammer). It is well known from experience that each throw must be built up from the legs. Problems with the base (the legs) decrease the range in each case. Figure 2 indicates in single positions the clear differences in the leg work (compare the knee and hip angles)

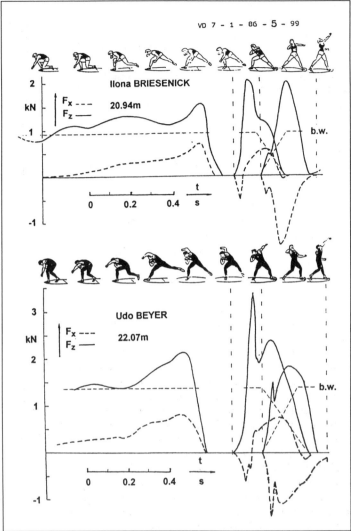

FIGURE 3: GROUND REACTION FORCES IN THE SHOT PUT (BARTONIETZ 1987)

partially responsible for the distances reached. It also shows the unity of skills and abilities.

We can often observe predominant work of the upper parts of a thrower's body with a bent left knee, a counter-movement of the lower part of the trunk (hips are set back) and a flat angle of release. It is necessary to understand

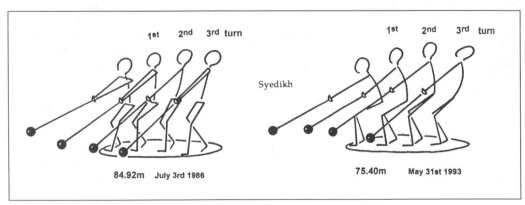

FIGURE 2: POSITION OF THE THROWER (LOWEST POINT OF THE HAMMER PATH) GOING INTO THE FIRST TURN AND DURING THE TURNS OVER A TIME PERIOD.

here the correct coordination. Biomechanical knowledge of the event is needed for correction of faults and for learning to take place.

During the delivery, the roles of the right and left leg work are exactly opposite: the right leg gives an accelerating impetus to the body and the left leg reduces the velocity (javelin, discus, shot) as much as possible. In the javelin, the bracing left leg work starts after the acceleration of the right; in the shot, discus and hammer the right acts against the left leg. Figure 3 illustrates these roles of the leg work, showing two different actions from the platform data:

- with very effective employment of the left leg (see above: an extended bracing left leg), the vertical component of the ground reaction forces more than doubles that of the the body weight, and

- with an inferior body tension as a result of a bending left knee, the vertical force component from the left leg is clearly lower.

Not shown in Figure 3 are the calculations from the platform data together with data from video analysis showing that the necessary power level (power as energy per time unit) for the bracing of the left leg is sometimes higher than for the right leg. It can be explained simply that the working capacity of the left leg limits the volume of throwing exercises within one training unit. Therefore the working capacity of the left leg is one of the key points in training.

An insight into the structure of the leg performance is available from the data of testing machines like Cybex (US), Kin-Trex (Swi) and others. Figure 4 shows the maximum of the force momentums of the hip, knee and ankle extensions and flexions of discus throwers (on the right a young woman discus thrower, in the center a junior, and on the left a world-class male athlete).

The junior reached values comparable to the world-class athlete (hips, knees) but threw about 15m shorter because his release velocity was about 3m/s slower. This testing indicated that young athletes need to develop a more balanced relation between flexors and extensors by sprinting and two- and one-legged jumping exercises, and through more specific strength and power training.

This data also gives a picture of the power output of the joint flexors and extensors, because in rotational movements the power is calculated by force momentum and angular velocity. For given angular velocities (like 60 deg/s in Figure 4), the momentum is proportional to the power.

It should be noted that the performance of the ankle impetus has a key function in all throwing events. The ankle must compensate for the effects from upper body, hip and knees (Newton: *actio et reactio*) and, additionally, must give its own impetus. The data in Figure 4 shows a low performance by the young thrower's ankle in relation to the hips and knees.

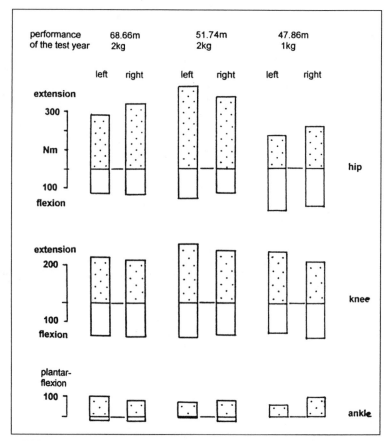

FIGURE 4: TEST DATA FROM THE KIN-TREX SYSTEM (60°/S)

The effectiveness of the glide in relation to the rotational technique in the shot put is easier to understand based on the analysis of the power demands. The power demands of the rotational technique are higher (about 20% for comparable ranges) because the path of the shot and the thrower's body during the delivery is shorter and the velocity of the shot is lower at the beginning of the delivery (Bartonietz 1983, 1990).

But the athlete can create the conditions for the necessary conversion of kinetic energy per time unit (power) with the help of leg work. This provides the base for an explosive angular acceleration of the upper body, creating a necessarily very high muscular pre-tension.

For this reason, there must be some differences in specific power training between gliders and spinners. The rotational technique is unlike the glide in that it is very difficult to perform without special preparations. And use of the rotational technique is by no means a must, as the performances of Ulf Timmermann have shown that the glide has not been exhausted.

2. LEARNING THE RIGHT TECHNIQUE AND AN EFFECTIVE CORRECTION OF FAULTS

Only a small number of recent top throwers have realized the demand for an approach to an ideal technique. To be among the world's best throwers doesn't mean automatically that one has an effective technique.

Take Andrey Abduvaliyev, who won the 1992 Olympic hammer throw with an 82.54m effort. A few months after the Games his defective technique still yielded throws over 80m.

His biomechanical parameters, shown in Table 1, reveal among other aspects a later catching of the hammer from turn to turn and therefore a shortening of the double-support phases in relation to the single-support phases.

TABLE 1: BIOMECHANICAL PARAMETERS OF AN 81.20M THROW BY A. ABDUVALIYEV (MAY 31, 1993)

Turns Parameter Duration(s)	1st	2nd	3rd	4th
Single support	0.32	0.26	0.26	0.26
Double support	0.38	0.26	0.18	0.20 (!)
Position catching the hammer	235°	245°	255°	280°
Inclination of the hammer plane	30°	36°	41°	46°
Angle of release				40°

Coaches and athletes must get a clear picture of the source of the faults when analyzing technique and detecting faults. The following factors are noteworthy:

- **Effective Learning and Improvement of Technique**

The initiation of changes when learning and improving technique can be rather complicated because most of the recent textbooks use illustrations of real athletes with their individual peculiarities and, in some cases, noticeable faults.

One of the important factors to emphasize is a reproducible and effective starting position for the delivery in all throwing events, as deviations from an effective starting position or the movements preceding the release are often a cause for faulty deliveries:

Javelin— decreasing the runup speed during the last strides, cross (or impulse) stride too short.
Consequences: upper body too upright when the right foot is planted, insufficient time for throwing preparation.

Shot put— starting the glide with a predominantly swinging movement of the left leg (supported by the left arm).
Consequences: not a glide but a jump, long amortization with great loss of velocity, premature movement of the upper body (lower pre-tension).

Discus— careless action going into the turn over the left leg.

Consequences: clear jumping movement with a fall of the right leg, missing of the torque for turning on the ball after planting the right foot in the middle of the circle, planting the left leg too late.

Hammer— shortening of a maximally wide hammer path going into the first turn.
Consequences: shortening of the hammer's radius during the turns leading to a shortening of the hammer's path of acceleration.

The improvement of the delivery must therefore start with finding the above mentioned sources for faults and not by identifying the final manifestation. Coaches must here have a clear internal picture of the technique; athletes need knowledge about the interplay of movements. They must *see* the desired key positions (for example, with the help of stick figures as in Figure 5) and *feel* these by imitation and other training exercises.

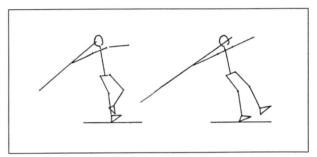

FIGURE 5: THE BODY POSITION AFTER PLANTING OF THE RIGHT FOOT AFTER THE IMPULSE STRIDE. LEFT—TRAINING THROW OF 85m. RIGHT—A DEFECTIVE POSITION AS A GUIDE TO TECHNIQUE TRAINING.

- **Development of the Abilities Corresponding With Target Skills**

Improvement of leg work capacity through squats to develop knee and hip extensors often goes hand in hand with shortcomings in the bracing left leg work, or the reactive power capacity of the ankle. Also, successful athletes often open a "gap" between the performances of training exercises and the competition movement.

This isn't the result of an ineffective "transformation" of general abilities to specific abilities. Rather, a transformation can't take place because specific abilities are not developed. The realized forces are the result of a given power level and not the source of the performance. Consequently, the conclusion for top athletes must be *more specificity in all spheres of training.*

The realization of this motto can be seen in Figure 6. It includes increased specificity in:

- an increase of throwing loads in comparison to

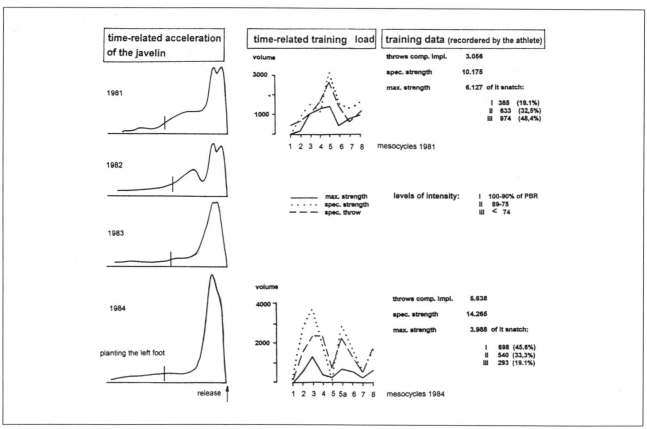

FIGURE 6: THE FINAL JAVELIN ACCELERATION OF PETRA FELKE AND THE MAIN ASPECTS OF HER TRAINING OVER TWO YEARS (BARTONIETZ 1992, BASED ON DATA FROM SCHULER).

strength training loads,

• the use of exercises that correspond to the demands of the competition exercise (short and explosive snatches, squats with a final extension of the ankle, etc.),

• a growing quality of technique training.

• **Adaptation to Short-, Medium- and Long-Term Training Loads**

Each training exercise has an effect on the movement pattern of the competition exercise (on the movement structure). This effect depends on the movement pattern of the training exercise. The interaction of different training exercises and loads for days and weeks produces the final adaptation.

Problems with the competition implement after throwing heavy implements is a well-known factor when specific training loads are employed. Such short-term adaptations are deliberate. Real problems start only when the athlete develops a stable bending knee or, in other words, when the so called "heavy implement technique" becomes stabilized for the athlete. An external sign of such an occurrence is a small difference between the distances thrown with competition and heavy implements.

In all throwing events, heavy implements create de-

viations from the competition movement (Bartonietz/Hellmann 1985, Bartonietz 1987). There is a tendency towards a shortening of the path of the implement's acceleration because the weakest "motors" are located at the end of the open kinetic chain.

As a positive effect, the greater inertia of such implements can create a higher pre-tension (however, the velocity is necessarily lower) for a more powerful delivery. In throwing these implements, though, the work of the left leg can be ineffective (bent left knee), if the leg power level is too low or the load too heavy. This leads to some deviation from the target coordination of the movements.

High demands on the technique, particularly on the leg work, are necessary in the use of heavy implements. Keep in mind also that the potential training effects of a given exercise are not automatic, and the target directed *execution of movements* plays an important role.

Athletes and coaches must take into consideration the increasing difficulties of developing technique after several years of training with improved strength capacities. However, the achievement of changes is possible, as shown in Figure 6, representing the training of Petra Felke. Her training was directed to improve conditions for the delivery, especially a more pronounced delay of the throw.

In the classification of training exercises in different training cycles (strength training, training of specific power, special throwing training), it is necessary to take into consideration the movement pattern and the specific training effect of these exercises (the movement structure).

3. RECOMMENDATIONS FOR TRAINING

• Skills and capacities form a given unit. There is no technique without capacities, and no capacities without technique. This is the leading principle for strength and technique training.

• Knowledge about effective technique is a must for coaches and athletes.

• The athlete needs realizable guidelines for individual movement patterns in order to positively orient technique training.

• Improvement and correction of technique demands the consideration of the total training contents.

• Heavy implements should always be used together with competition implements, taking into consideration the individual performance level. Implements that are too heavy lead to negative results. Also, the technical demands must be stressed in the use of heavy implements.

• Varying the mass of implements used prevents undesired adaptations.

• Set higher demands for the work of the bracing left leg by using higher movement velocity in the preparation phases (runup glide, turn and heavy implements or additional resistances such as vests, cuffs, etc).

• Reduce the number of throws from the standing position. They have a place only in a special warmup. Use standing throws only in the target-directed work of the left leg.

WORLD RECORD HOLDER PETRA FELKE

CHAPTER II: THE SHOT

MODEL TECHNIQUE ANALYSIS SHEETS FOR THROWING EVENTS— THE SHOT PUT

by Günter Tidow, Germany

A detailed biomechanical analysis of shot put technique based on the linear approach of the O'Brien glide.

1. Introduction

The statement that the rotational technique is a genuine alternative to the linear technique is only true as far as the preliminary acceleration of the "putter-implement" system is concerned. In any case, the starting position (with hips and shoulders square to the rear), level of acceleration and power position of the rotational technique are closely related to the O'Brien technique or even derived from it. Therefore, in this article and the accompanying analysis sheet, the phases of the "original" linear technique will be presented and discussed as a basis, as it were.

In Figure 1, the reader is given a general impression of the O'Brien technique.

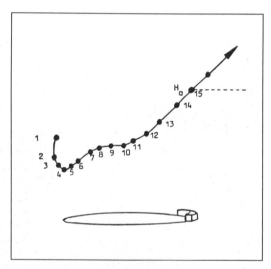

FIGURE 2
The path of the shot in a 20m put. This put is the basis of the technique model described in the analysis sheet. Each numbered dot represents the position of the shot in the respective movement phase in chronological order.
- Phase 4: starting squat
- Phase 7: beginning of glide
- Phase 9: power position
- Phase 15: delivery.
In phase 4—i.e. the lowest point of the path—the shot is approx. 82cm above the level of the circle. It is delivered at a height of 227cm. The angle of release is 41°, the preliminary acceleration path (phase 4 to 9) is 90cm long, and the main acceleration path (phase 9 to 14) is 182cm long. Between phase 4 to 9, the shot is lifted 36cm; from phase 9 to the delivery "lift" is 109cm (athlete's body height: 1,90m).

FIGURE 1: The O'Brien technique divided into 17 phases (athlete: P. Shmock [USA])

2. Starting position and preliminary movement

The initial phases serve to lower the total "athlete-shot" system. The "starting point" of the diagonally rising acceleration path is only reached with the transition from phase 3 to phase 4 (see Figure 2). The downward directed preliminary phases (phases 1 to 3) will not be discussed in detail here, the reasons being:

- there is no significant relationship between the quality of the preliminary phases and the throwing distance;

- there have always been athletes who, after the preliminary phase, "rest" for a short time in the so-called starting squat and only then really start the glide from this low position.

Although a fluent overlapping of the preliminary phases and the beginning of the glide seems to be more efficient and to lead to a lighter load on the supporting leg, these aspects seem to be relatively insignificant taking into account the strength levels of current specialists and the transmission losses that must be compensated for after the glide.

Therefore, the use or non-use of the T-position—which scarcely influences the shot path—will not be further dealt with here. The comparison of both preliminary phases presented in Figure 3 shows that both variants lead to an identical crouch position, called the starting crouch.

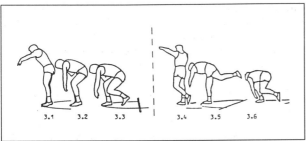

FIGURE 3: the preliminary movement with (3.1 to 3.3) and without T-position (3.4 to 3.6). In both cases, the total system is lowered against the (normal) throwing direction in order to get into the "starting crouch" (see 3.3 or 3.6). In this position, the "first one-legged support phase" is begun, which is also the starting point for the diagonally upward directed path of the shot.

Doubtlessly, not using the T-position is the more direct way to attain the crouch position and although the two-footed position at the rear of the circle gives the athlete a greater feeling of security, there are some points which favor use of the T-position. It anticipates the extension of the swinging leg—which is necessary at the beginning of the glide—on a "higher level," as it were. This results in a preliminary rhythm that can easily be performed, particularly by learners: extension (into the T-position)—lowering (into the starting crouch)—extension (action of the swinging leg at the beginning of the glide).

As already mentioned, all this is unimportant as far as top level athletes are concerned; it should, however, be taken into account when teaching the glide to beginners.

3. From the starting crouch to the beginning of the glide

The starting crouch is a favorable position for the putter to direct the line of propulsion of the implement right from the start to the optimal angle of release and to accelerate the total system efficiently. This is done primarily by a "low" vigorous use of the swinging leg in the direction of the stopboard, which leads to this leg's complete or almost complete extension. The term "low" is used because, deviating from the original O'Brien technique, the knee of the swinging leg is no longer moved to the knee of the support leg, but to the calf (see Figure 4.1).

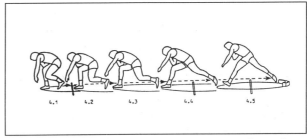

FIGURE 4: The first one-legged support phase from the starting crouch (4.1) to the beginning of the glide (4.5).

So an almost flat push backward of the (lower) swinging leg, which is almost parallel to the ground, is possible. This action of the swinging leg, which through the pull at the pelvis leads to a backward and downward movement of the total system, is partially overlapped by the pushoff of the gliding leg. This pushoff is done vigorously and is aided by the downward pull of gravity. In other words: the impulse of the swinging leg, which is directed diagonally downward, triggers a "fall" backwards, which is actively enforced by the almost simultaneous extension of the driving leg (abbreviated by "g" on the analysis sheet). The result of this "joint action" of swinging and driving leg, as well as gravitation, is the taking up of another sort of T-position that, contrary to the T-position mentioned above, is "tilted" toward the stopboard (see Figure 4.5). This tilt is caused by the fact that (normally) contact is broken at the back of the circle by the heel (see Figure 4.5). This position is sometimes called the A-position.

If the free arm is held downward in front of the body, it is guaranteed that the "closed" trunk position of the starting crouch is not changed (see Figures 4.1 to 4.5). This is very important because the shot—as well as the shoulder axis—must stay behind the pelvis when, during the glide, it is rotated 90° in the direction of the throw. This rotation of the pelvis is anticipated as it were by a slightly outward turned foot of the swinging leg (see Figure 4.5). This means that the extended swinging leg performs a slight outward rotation so that the foot is grounded (at the stopboard) in the optimal position.

4. From the beginning of the glide to the power position

The fact that, in the O'Brien technique, the path of the shot can be divided into three phases, as indicated in Figure 2, inevitably results in a deviation from the theoretically ideal straight line path of propulsion.

The "curved path," demonstrated in Figure 2, is primarily caused by the fact that the excellent, diagonally upward directed phases of preliminary acceleration (phases 4 to 7; see also Figure 4) and the corresponding phases of final acceleration (phases 10 to 14) are connected by a midphase. This midphase is represented by the contourograms in Figure 5.

FIGURE 5: From the beginning of the glide (5.1) to the power position (5.3).

The main cause of this "saddle" (cf., Gehrmann 1981) is that the first positive acceleration phase is completed when phase 7, which is shown in Figure 5.1, is reached and the "passive" (when compared with the velocity curve of the total system) glide begins. It would be possible to achieve a quasi linear continuation of the first path of propulsion, by a continuous rising of the trunk during this phase of support without drive. However, such a movement behavior—which is sometimes demonstrated even by top level putters—would inevitably lead to a relatively high position of the shot in the following performance-determining power position. The power position is decisive for throwing performance, since 90% of the distance thrown with a glide can be reached from the standing position alone. A shortened acceleration path in the power position would certainly offset the advantage resulting from the almost linear rise of the shot.

So the gliding phase—in the course of which the shot travels about 30cm and is accelerated to 2 to 3 m/sec (cf., Ballreich & Kuhlow 1986)—is primarily used for two other tasks. The first task is to cause a rotation of the pelvis by contraction of the oblique trunk muscles, until the pelvic axis points exactly in the normal throwing direction. This leads to a pre-stretching of the antagonistic oblique external and internal (abdominal) muscles.

When taking up the power position, the shot putter is therefore in a "torqued state"." The build-up of this torque is made possible through a strong "freezing" of the trunk position during the glide. The "closing" action of the free arm against the throwing direction (see Figures 5.1 to 5.3) supports this movement. From this it follows that, in the case of an optimal performance of the glide, the shoulder axis remains square to the normal throwing direction until the foot of the swinging leg hits the ground right in front of the stopboard.

This can, however, only be realized if this (front) foot is grounded almost synchronously with the rear foot (as demonstrated in Figure 5). Only then can the "transition phase" (cf., Bauersfeld & Schroeter 1986) be left out. The term "transition phase" is used for describing the time interval between the landing of the gliding foot in the center of the circle and the grounding of the swinging foot at the stopboard.

As early as 1972, top class putters showed a tendency to shorten this phase (cf., Kuhlow & Heger 1975). If, right at the beginning of the glide, the swinging leg is flatly and accurately directed to the stopboard, the "landing-asynchrony"—and together with this the transition phase—can be reduced to a few milliseconds at the most. Only when this occurs can the driving leg take up its turn-push function against the resistance of the left leg without loss of time.

Next, during the glide, the rear leg must pass rapidly from full extension to flexion, in order to get into an effective position as a driving force, once the power position is reached. This flexing coincides with the rotation of the hips described above. The movement produced in this process resembles an "underswing" that is performed actively and fast by the lower part of the rear leg with a simultaneous inward rotation of the foot. At the same time, this foot is tilted downwards. At the beginning of the glide, the last contact with the surface of the circle was made by the heel, but it is the ball of the foot that first contacts the ground at the end of the glide.

In order to avoid frictional losses and braking effects during the glide—in the course of which the rear foot travels about 70cm (measured from the heel to the tip of the foot)—a low, shallow hop (as presented in Figure 5.2) is more useful than a continuous contact with the ground as is suggested by the term "glide."

5. From the power position to the sideways putting position

The primary function of the glide is to shift the total system to the front half of the circle. The secondary function is to achieve an optimal position for the following main acceleration.

The power position provides the putter's effective stance. The term "power position" implies an immediate, explosive effect on the shot. On closer examination, however, the situation is different. A further reason for the deviation of the shot from the ideal path mentioned above is the fact that the putter must delay the "lifting" of the shot until he has shifted his pelvis (through a turning and pushing action of his rear leg) into the "bridge position." Only when both legs have firm contact with the ground and the free leg can fulfill its resisting function at the stopboard, may the athlete—while continuing to turn and push—begin to raise his trunk and the shot.

The clearly visible rise of the shot in phase 11 (see Figure 6.3) indicates this process. The importance of the turn and push is based on functional-anatomical reasons: only a two-legged, firm support allows the athlete to conserve or even intensify the pre-tension of the trunk that has

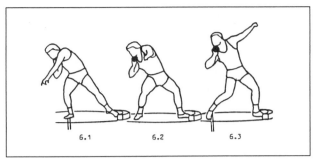

FIGURE 6

been achieved in the power position.

Here the shift, caused by the primarily horizontally directed turn and push, must first be applied to the pelvis so that the trunk remains low and behind the "driving" leg when the bridge position has been achieved. Only in this way can three separate tasks be optimally fulfilled:

1. The putter must perform a pivoting movement in order to move from the back to the frontal position.

2. The putter must also perform a lift and extension movement in order to achieve the optimal release angle of the shot.

3. The putter must shift his bodyweight in order to move from the power position ("from the rear and low") to the throwing position ("to the front and high").

The difficulty is that all of these tasks must "actually" be effected at the same time.

The "overlapping" of the shift, pivot and lift resulting from this cannot be altered as far as their sequence is concerned: the horizontal shift and rotational movement of the pelvis during the glide are immediately continued by the rear leg as it lands in the power position. The turn-push that is necessary for this takes the athlete into the bridge position and after this into the sideways position.

Many athletes, such as Werner Günthör (SWI), make this a turn-tilt-push, because the leg extension can produce acceleration only if the knee is in front of the foot. The trunk, which, in the power position, was quite low and behind the driving leg, "follows" this change of position.

FIGURE 7: Turn-push of the gliding leg and "diagonal rise" of the free arm. These two actions take place almost simultaneously.

The active raising of the free arm supports this simultaneously performed turn-push movement. The process described here becomes clear if one compares the position of the free arm and driving leg in the power position (see Figure 7.1) with that in the sideways position (see Figure 7.3).

In order to avoid an early "opening," the putter should direct his eyes toward the rear during the turn-push. In doing so, he avoids the "running forward" of his putting shoulder. Correspondingly, the perpendicular projection of the center of gravity of the shot should meet the ground near the driving foot, which guarantees an effective and long "shoulder hit" from the sideways position (see Figure 8).

FIGURE 8
Sideways positon as starting position for the "lift." The arrows show that the lines of the shoulder axis, putting and free arm as well as the lower part of the driving leg are now parallel. Even here, their direction is identical with the release angle.

If one considers again the path of the shot presented in Figure 1, it becomes obvious that only in the sideways position a lifting movement starts that is exactly directed to the release angle. This leads to the conclusion that the sequence of shift, pivot and lift mentioned above is indeed true.

Beginning the lift immediately after having reached the power position by an extension of the driving leg (particularly favored by putters whose trunk muscles are not so strong) results in a decrease of performance: a good bridge position cannot be developed in this way. Correspondingly, it is inevitable that the main acceleration phase becomes a "one-legged put. A possible pre-tension of the trunk cannot be conserved or made use of since the front foot only touches the ground lightly and for a very short time.

The result is that this leg can neither be used as a lever nor as a driving force for the explosive final extension of the whole body . The immediate, vertical extension of the driving leg also leads to neglect of the pivoting movement. Consequently, the trunk must be used as a "motor" that pulls the lower body along with it. This is, however, a perversion of the correct movement process.

The solution regarding the behavior of the driving leg presented here has been disputed for a long time. So Werner (cf., Werner 1965) and Heger (cf., Kuhlow & Heger 1975) favor the vertical extension of the driving leg while Grigalka, (cf., Grigalka 1980) recommended that the extension of this leg ". . . should be simply forbidden."

However, the statement made by Lindner as early as 1967 remains irrefutable, namely that the parallel curve of shot and pelvis in the movement phase under discussion is characteristic of "the less qualified putting technique," whereas specialists demonstrate a rather opposite trend. This means that, in the case of specialists, the shot rises while the pelvis is slightly lowered (cf., Lindner 1967).

This finding at least indirectly confirms the justification of Grigalka's "ban on the extension of the rear leg" in the movement segment under discussion.

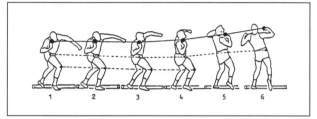

FIGURE 9: Movement behavior and resulting characteristic lines of the shot, pelvis and the knee from the power position to the delivery position. The comparison of the lines makes their opposite course obvious (figure according to Tidow, 1983)

Figure 9 was constructed in order to verify this statement. The characteristic lines in this figure have been drawn on the basis of a put by the former Olympic gold medalist and world record holder Randy Matson (USA). The comparison of the lines shows that, at the beginning, the path of the shot runs parallel to the ground (phases 1 to 3). Then it rises slightly (phases 3 and 4) and finally steeply, while, simultaneously, the pelvis and the knee of the driving leg move slightly downward.

Doubtlessly, the cause of this is the turn-push of the driving leg, as has been mentioned several times in this article. A vertically upward directed extension of this leg, during this phase at the start of the power position, cannot be seen in the majority of the current top level shot putters.

The occasional persistence of an immediate extension impulse is, apart from strength deficits, perhaps also caused by a wrong over-emphasis on the standing put, both during the learning stages and in technique training.

It goes without saying that the quasi "static conditions" of the standing put make a basically different, primarily vertical use of the rear leg appear sensible. Much repetition of the standing put could lead to the development of a motor stereotype that could also show itself in gliding puts.

In any case, it is considerably easier to perform the turn-push when some momentum has been gained. This note should, however, not hide the fact that, even in standing puts, the athlete must also perform the initial "shifting work" in a primarily horizontal direction.

6. From the sideways stance to the delivery

The sideways stance, which, in fact, can be observed only for a very short time, is the starting position for the explosive-ballistic final acceleration of the shot. Since at this moment the acceleration of the trunk is greater than that of the pelvis, the torque between shoulder and pelvic axis is released during the lift. So in the frontal position—

which from now on is called "delivery position"—both axes are parallel to each other and vertically above each other.

The explosive extension of the putting arm should take place only after the abrupt stopping of the free arm, which had been pulled diagonally upwards. This abrupt stopping produces an additional positive acceleration of the putting shoulder. After the energetic "pull upward" along the line of the release angle, the free arm is bent at the elbow and fixed at the side of the trunk. In Figure 10 this movement process is presented in three phases.

It becomes obvious that the demand made above that the putting arm should only be extended when the putter's breast/shoulder axis is square to the (normal) putting direction is not fulfilled completely (see Figure 10). The premature opening of the elbow joint of the putting arm, which is already indicated in phase 10.3, is sometimes more pronounced in the case of throws between 21 and 23m. It is unlikely that this is a simple fault. The presently achieved load-strength relationship might, rather, be so favorable that an ideal arm movement, i.e., an arm movement that is optimal as far as timing is concerned (see Figure 11), could even lead to a reduction of distance.

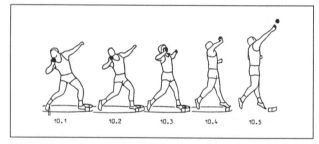

FIGURE 10: From the sideways stance (10.1) through the delivery position (10.3) to the actual delivery (10.5). The movement section depicted here takes only 150ms. Sideways stance and frontal position (10.3) are therefore only very short "transition phases."

FIGURE 11: "Ideal" delivery position from side and rear. Figure 11.1 shows the pre-tension of the chest muscles and the still clearly bent putting arm, which has been lifted to shoulder height. Here, putting hand and shot are in front of the shoulder.

Since nowadays the best putters are able to perform one-arm lifts with 100kg weights (bench press), 7.25kg shots are in the area of 7% (!) of the maximal strength of the putting arm. If the relative explosive strength has been optimally developed under these conditions, it at least seems to be possible to coincide the delivery movement with the shoulder hit.

Regardless of the time of innervation and the speed of contraction of the extensor muscles of the arm, it is an elementary rule to lift the elbow of the putting arm at least to shoulder height after the shot has passed the shoulder (see Figures 10.1 to 10.5 and Figure 11).

The reason for this rule is that the raised elbow guarantees that the whole body stays behind the implement all through the delivery action. It also permits a final impulse to be given to the shot by means of a "horizontal" volar flexion of the wrist (see Figure 12).

FIGURE 12: The release of the shot. Here the elbow of the putting arm is lifted, and the wrist of the putting hand is in volar flexion. This movement is directed horizontally and outward.

If the putter imagines that there is, directly beside or in front of him, a shoulder high ball of foam material which he is not allowed to contact with his putting arm, he will generally succeed in achieving the correct high elbow position. However, this is only true if sufficient torque has been built up in the power position and if this torque has not been released too early. The following fast swing of the shoulder axis into the delivery position will then press the shot into the putting hand firmly enough. Otherwise the elbow must be lowered to prevent the from shot falling from the hand.

During the delivery itself, the whole body should be extended (see Figure 13). In this way it is guaranteed that the final extension impulse of both legs, which is mainly vertical, really "hits" the shot.

FIGURE 13: Delivery of the shot. The accentuated loss of contact with the ground shown in this figure is typical of the movement behavior of current top level shot putters.

A falling away or lowering of the hips would shatter this intention. In any case, the putting arm needs a firm support in order to utilize its power effectively. The locking of the free arm, already mentioned, is another essential element of the buildup of this support, which is completed by the firm locking of all trunk muscles. In this way, a too great rotation of the shoulder axis can be avoided, and a bending of the trunk toward the side of the free arm can be eliminated.

The required rapid extension of the whole body also contributes to the maximization of the release height. This parameter influences the throwing distance of the shot in direct proportion to height (cf., Ballreich & Kuhlow 1986).

Whether the delivery should be done with or without ground contact of at least the front support leg is hardly disputed any longer. It is also undisputable that, when "springing out the shot" (Nett 1969), the athlete's body must compensate, according to Newton's law, for the "action" of the putting arm. However, the disadvantage arising from this is obviously more than compensated for.

A delivery without ground support makes a dynamic follow-through possible because only then can the following reverse be performed with the whole body in the putting direction. Moreover it seems unavoidable for the shot putter to lose the contact with the ground just prior to the delivery, if the power and coordination of the extensor muscles of the leg and hips are to be fully exploited.

If one analyzes the movement behavior of the current top level shot putters, it becomes obvious that the majority deliver the shot having lost foot contact. In contrast to this, the result of the analysis of the women's shot put is not so uniform.

Hypothetically it can be assumed that with the women, because of a clearly more favorable strength-load relationship (bodyweight approximately 85kg/shot weight 4kg = 21:1, as compared to 116 kg/7.26kg = 16:1), the acceleration conditions are different. This makes a slinging movement of the trunk, which is similar to that in the javelin throw, possible.

This slinging movement of the trunk is facilitated by a rangy power position with a strong pre-tension of the trunk and a "genuine" use of the bracing leg. This is particularly the case when the short-long rhythm is used.

The fact that some female shot putters do not lift the elbow of their putting arms higher than their shoulder further supports the assumption that the difference in the men's and women's movement behavior mentioned above is indeed true.

Whether these characteristics can be attributed to different teaching methods must remain an open question. The fact that in many countries—but not everywhere— there are men's and women's shot put coaches who, separately from each other, rather intuitively develop optimal movement patterns and variants of solution in close cooperation with their athletes supports and explains the tendency for differentiation mentioned above.

8. Delivery and reverse

The explosive extension of the leg, which leads to the

delivery of the shot, and the long shoulder hit almost automatically lead to the reverse. During the reverse, the rear leg is brought forward to a spot close to the stopboard where, just prior to this, the foot of the front leg has been. The main function of this movement behavior is to avoid stepping over the stopboard. However, additionally, this movement makes a dynamic follow-through possible (see Figure 14).

FIGURE 14: From the delivery of the shot to the reverse (on the left from the rear view, on the right from the side view).

The springing out of the shot and the following change of leg position must be seen as a unit. When the short-long rhythm is used, the reverse is not so necessary or can even be left out completely. The reason for this is that the wide support, and correspondingly more pronounced bracing function of the front leg, in this technique effectively slows down the forward and upward shift of the total system.

9. Summary

The phases or phase elements presented, as well as the corresponding assessment criteria of the modern O'Brien technique are summed up in the shot put analysis sheet. Since what is observed is to a great extent dependent on the onlooker's position (cf., Tidow 1983), it is recommended that the shot putter should be observed not only from the side but also from the rear.

Here, further details, such as the behavior of the putting arm from the initial position at the back of the circle (including the correct hold and position of the shot at the neck) to the delivery can be closely observed.

The judging of the position of the feet in relation to each other (in the power position, criterium: "15cm staggered") demanded in phase element 23 requires the view from the rear. Only from the rear is it possible to see the degree of sideways deviation of the front foot from the normal putting position (in relation to the rear foot).

Since, in the linear shot put technique, the movements are presented in a period of between 800 and 1000 milliseconds, it is necessary to concentrate on only two to three details per attempt or only on certain faults.

However, as far as consideration of the technique model is concerned, and in the diagnosis of the filmed movement sequence, the analysis sheet should be used in a complex way, i.e., from phase to phase and on the element level as well.

REFERENCES

BALLREICH. R., KUHLOW, A.: *Biomechanik des Kuge/stoßes.* In: Biomechanik der Sponarten. Vol. 1: Biomechanik der Leichtathletik. Stuttgart 1986, 89- 109.

BAUERSFELD, K.-H., SCHROETER, G.: *Grundlagen der Leichtathletik.* Berlin (East) 1986.

BOSEN, K.O.: *Comparative Study Between the Conventional and the Rotational Techniques of Shot Put.* In: Athletics Asia 1 (1984).

GEHRMANN, C.: *Uberlegungen und Erfahrungen zum Kugelstoßtraining.* In: AUGUSTIN, D., MULLER, N. (Ed.): Leichtathletiktraining. Niedernhausen 1981.

GRIGALKA, O.: *Zur Technik des Kugelstoßes.* LdLa 23 (1980), 667-670 and 24 (1980), 699-702.

HOMMEL, H.: *Lehrbildreihe Nr. 968 (Pete Shmock, USA).* In: LdLa 6 (1981), 236-237.

HOKE, R.J.: *Geschichte und technische Entwicklung des Kugelstossens.* In: LdLa 47 (1966), l489-l492 and 48 (1966), 1538.

KUHLOW, A., HEGER, W.: *Die Technik des Kugelstoßens der Männer bei den Olympischen Spielen 1972 in München.* Beiheft "Leistungssport" 2 (1975).

LINDNER. E.: *Sprung und Wurf.* Schomdorf 1967.

NETT, T.: *Die Technik beim Stoß und Wurf.* Berlin (West) 1961.

NETT, T.: *Kernphasen der Kugelsoßtechnik.* In: LdLa 26 (1969) 907/910 and 27 (1969) 945/947 f.

TIDOW, G.: *Der Einfluß pädagogischer Aspekte auf den Zehnkampf.* In: DLV-Kongressbericht "Mehrkampf." Ed.: HOMMEL, H. Darmstadt 1978, 17-21.

TIDOW, G.: *Modell zur Technikschulung und Bewegungsbeurteilung in der Leichtathletik.* In: Leistungssport 4 (1981), 264-277.

TIDOW, G.: *Beobachtung und Beurteilung azyklischer Bewegungsabläufe.* Ahrensburg: Czwalina 1983.

TSCHIENE, P.: *Eine neue Auffassung von der Technik des Kugelstoßens?* In: LdLa 17 (1973), 593-596.

WERNER, E.: *Nur dosiertes Hanteltraining führt zum Erfolg.* In: LdLa 3 (1965), 71-72.

WILT, F.: *Shot Putting Analyzed.* In: The Scholastic Joumal 8 (1977), 46-47.

ZACIORSKIJ, W.N.: *Biomechanische Probleme des Kugelstoßens.* In: Leistungssport 2 (1980), 132-142.

SOME BIOMECHANICAL OBSERVATIONS OF THE ROTATIONAL SHOT PUT

by Vello Palm, Estonia

A summary of a biomechanical analysis of the rotational shot put technique with a comparison of the actions employed by Barishnikov and Bojars.

The introduction of novel techniques in track & field often generates a mixed reaction from specialists. Such reactions were evident with the introduction of the flop technique in the high jump and the rotational shot put technique. Even though some of the world's best athletes used these innovative techniques, their success was not considered sufficient proof in favor of their adoption as a general model for all athletes.

When Barishnikov achieved 19.20m with the shot put method involving a turn (the spin) in the early 1970s, most of the specialists were doubtful about the prospect of this technique. His world record (22.00m) set in 1976 forced many of them to change their views, and a number of athletes such as Oldfield (22.86m), Laut (22.02), Melnikova (20.21m) and others adopted this method.

Specialists began to study and analyze the essence of the rotational method, basing their studies on film sequences and analysis of the speed and trajectory of the shot. These studies were carried out on one plane in a two dimensional space. It was concluded that, in comparison with the conventional glide technique of Feuerbach, no advantage was gained by the rotational method. The main conclusion was that the athlete achieves shot velocities of about 4 to 5m/sec with the rotational acceleration but that shot velocity decreases at the start of the delivery phase to 0.5m/sec, hence negating the value of this method.

However, observations by outstanding specialists in the field (Alekseyev, Grigalka, Voronia, et al.) soon gave us reason to assume that, if athletes and coaches were to perfect the technique of rotational acceleration, the method could be more advantageous.

The mastery of rotational shot technique requires an understanding of movement regulations of the system of bodies which includes the shot. This facilitates the design of purposeful training processes and the development of a technique based on biomechanical principles that are reflected in the athlete's motion dynamics. In this article we have used the methods developed by Krevald in 3-dimensional analysis of sporting techniques.

THREE-DIMENSIONAL ANALYSIS

In this method, two synchronized film cameras are used to record the motion of the athlete and the shot in order to produce a 3-dimensional picture of the movement. Calculations were performed using a Data-Saab D-5/30 computer using the following coordinate system:

z-axis: vertically directed

y-axis: longitudinal axis (direction of throw)

x-axis: direction perpendicular to the direction of the put.

Biomechanical quantities such as the angular momentum of the entire system and linear momentum are quite informative in the 3-dimensional motion studies of the athlete-shot system. Momentum is the measure of the forward motion of a body which is characterized by its ability to convey mechanical movement to another body. It is measured by the product of the body mass and its velocity ($\vec{K} = m \times \vec{v}$).

Angular momentum is a measure of the rotational movements of a body which are characterized by the ability to convey velocity to another body in the form of mechanical movement. Angular momentum is equal to the tensor of the moment of inertia relative to the axis of rotation and the angular velocity of the body (L - lw).

First analysis of Barishnikov's action with a 10kg shot revealed that the rotational method of acceleration of the shot differs radically from the common glide technique and provides opportunities to improve performances. Studies of Melnikova's putting in 1982 (20.21m) confirmed similarities in the investigated parameters to the technique of Barishnikov in the dynamics of the modulus (absolute size) of the quantity vector of the shot. The analysis revealed that the maximal shot velocity during the acceleration (2.87m/sec) indeed decreased at the start of the delivery phase to 0.58m/sec (Figure 1). However the velocity of the shot at the release was 11.18m/sec.

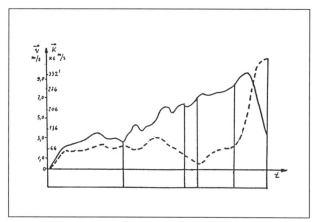

FIGURE 1: THE SHOT AND COMBINED MASS VELOCITIES—BARYSHNIKOV: 15.96m (10kg SHOT)

— — — — — SHOT VELOCITY ——————— MASS VELOCITY

Considering the changes of velocity in the combined mass, it can be seen that the modulus of the mass velocity sector increases during the process of the put. The vector modulus reaches its maximum (261.92kg m/sec) shortly before the delivery arm is activated.

The modulus of the quantity of the motion is applied in Figure 2 in comparison with the dynamics of a different method (Bojars, 20.60 in 1982). It is necessary to note that the weight of each athlete (Bojars and Barishnikov) was 125kg. As can be seen, the maximum velocity of the combined mass system was reached at the end of the single-support phase of the acceleration, after which the velocity decreased.

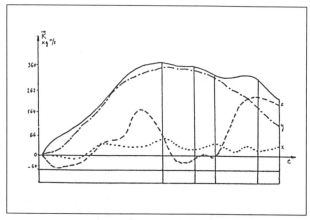

FIGURE 2: VELOCITY OF THE COMBINED MASS SYSTEM—BOJARS: 20.60m

Some increase in the quantity of the motion can be observed in the double-support phase of the delivery. This is noticeable in the z- but not the y-axis. A sharp decrease in the velocity of the mass takes place in the direction of the y-axis after the acceleration phase. This is not inten-

sively evident after the placement of the left foot. It is therefore possible to conclude that the athlete's motion after the acceleration phase takes place as the result of the energetic activities of the left leg (the quantity of the motion increases in the direction of the z-axis). At the moment of release of the shot the athlete is unsupported. All efforts are apparently directed to the vertical elevation of the system.

Unlike Bojars, Barishnikov is capable of increasing the quantity of the motion in the direction of the y-axis practically until the moment the putting arm is activated. The quantity of the motion in the direction of the z-axis is increased only to the extent required to prevent stepping over.

During the rotational acceleration of the combined system a relatively large and homogenous momentum is revealed (Figure 3), which is characteristic of rotational movements. The modulus of the vector achieves its maximum (130kg m/sec) at the release of the shot.

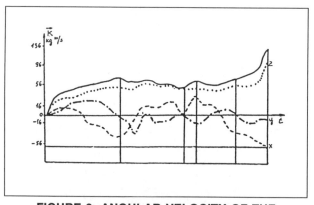

FIGURE 3: ANGULAR VELOCITY OF THE COMBINED MASS SYSTEM—BARYSHNIKOV: 15.96m (10kg SHOT)

During the final phase of acceleration, the athlete uses a so-called rotational straightening of the right leg and the body. This leg action simultaneously lifts the body (angular momentum around the x-axis) towards the direction of the put and increases angular momentum of the system around the z-axis.

Considerably less angular momentum (127.20kg m2/sec) can be observed in the action of Bojars at the moment the shot is released (Figure 4). Consequently the rotation of the system around the x-axis (straightening of the right leg and body) is significant in increasing the angular momentum. The angular momentum of the system around the z-axis is smaller, as this occurs rotationally around the vertical axis of the center of the athlete's mass in the direction of the put. For Barishnikov, it reaches 115.85kg m2/sec at the delivery.

This short analysis makes it possible to make some methodological recommendations for utilization in training:

- The right leg activity is the decisive element in the acceleration (for right-handed athletes).

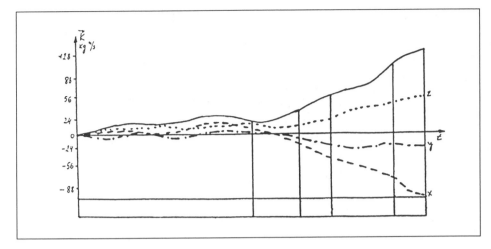

FIGURE 4: ANGULAR MOMENTUM OF THE COMBINED MASS SYSTEM— BOJARS: 20.60m

- The right foot must rest on the toes to secure continuous rotation around the vertical axis in the direction of the put during the contact with the circle.

- The entire acceleration must be performed in a relatively low position, without fluctuations in the y-plane.

- The athlete should, if possible, maximally accelerate the entire system in the direction of the put in the delivery phase (single and double support positions).

BALANCE IS THE KEY

Two related actions can be distinguished in the shot put technique—the gathering of momentum and the delivery. In order to give the shot the highest possible initial velocity, the athlete is forced to accelerate himself, as well as the total athlete-shot system. Practical experience has shown here that, if rotation in the circle is not performed in a balanced position, the shot is often delivered too early or in the wrong direction.

At the same time, however, the athlete makes a great effort to remain in the circle in order to avoid fouling. Obviously, a technique that requires the athlete to exploit valuable strength during the rotation to maintain balance is by no means optimal.

So-called inertia momentum is commonly used in mechanics to characterize the asymmetry of the distribution of masses. By drawing axes x, y and z through a point o, the centrifugal inertia momenta of these axes correspond to the magnitudes of lzy, lyz and lxz. The symmetry of the distribution of the masses relative to the z-axis is characterized by the centrifugal inertia momenta of lxz and lyz being equal to zero. In other words, the centrifugal inertia momenta of lxz and lyz indicate the state of the dynamic balance of the body masses rotating around the z-axis.

The centrifugal inertia momenta of lxy, lyz and lzx of the athlete-shot system were mathematically calculated for Barishnikov (15.96m, using a 10kg shot) and Melnikova (20.21m, using a 4kg shot). The results are graphically

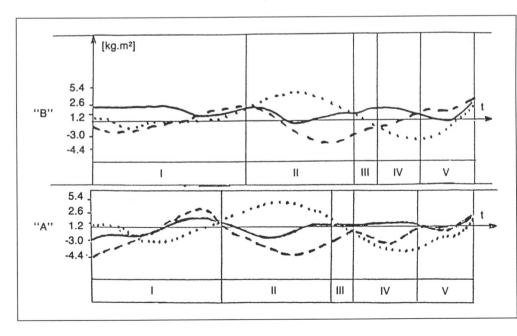

FIGURE 5: GRAPHICS OF THE CENTRIFUGAL INERTIA MOMENTS

A = Baryshnikov;
B = Melnikova;
1xy = ———;
1xz = ...;
1yz = - - - - - - - - - - -
I = Double Support Phase;
II = Single Support Phase;
III = Non-Support Phase;
IV = Single Support Phase;
V = Double Support Phase

Ziqurds Mezavilks

Brian Oldfield, one of the most successful of the rotational shot putters.

presented in Figure 5.

The graph shows that athlete "A" (Barishnikov) is in a perfectly balanced position in the beginning of first and second single support phases. The athlete can in these positions rationally apply force to the acceleration of the total athlete-shot system. The kinetic momentum of the system is increased.

The results of the analysis indicated that centrifugal inertia momenta lzy, lyz and lxz can objectively show the state of balance of the rotating system. The athlete will have to use a fair amount of his physical power to restore balance, even if the deviation takes place in only one direction (forward, backward or sideways).

CONCLUSIONS

The results of the analysis show that the essence of the rotational acceleration of the shot cannot be determined solely by the measurements of the velocity of the shot and its trajectory. The above-presented investigation reveals that the quantity of motion and kinetic energy do not decrease along with the velocity decreases of the shot.

To conclude, it can be stated that the calculated paramenters that characterize the dimensional motion of the shot and the entire system prove that the rotational technique is more economical and perhaps also more promising than the well-known versions of the O'Brien shift.

WHY HASN'T ROTATIONAL SHOT PUTTING TAKEN OFF IN THE SAME WAY THAT THE FOSBURY FLOP HAS?

by Carl Johnson, Great Britain

British master coach Johnson compares the progress rotational shot technique has made with the development of the flop technique in high jumping and examines the strengths and weaknesses of the rotational style.

The Fosbury Flop (the modern variant of many early attempts in high jumping to cash in on the advantages of a back layout) was eventually developed as the direct result of general advances in modern technology which made foam landing areas possible, and brought an innovative athlete to Olympic success in 1968.

Rotational shot putting came to notice four years later in 1972. Although authorities quote several instances of experimentation with similar concepts before that date, Alexander Baryshnikov (Russia) is recognized as its first important exponent. He threw 20.54 to rank 12th in the world, but could only place 22nd in the Olympic Games of that year. Even at his best he would not have been good enough to win medals at that competition.

It took him a further four years to annex a world record, and he, or the technique, were again not sufficiently sound enough to prevail in the Olympics of 1976. Rotational shot putting was thus denied the high profile impact that Fosbury had been able to ensure with his new form of high jumping in 1968.

Perhaps the technique did get off to a poor start, but I quote former colleague Peter Lay, who wrote in the BAAB 1972 Olympic report "Oldfield (at the American Olympic Trials) switched to the Baryshnikov technique and landed at 21.92m . . . We will see more of this technique in the future—Brian Oldfield has seen to that."

Perhaps Baryshnikov was not a Dick Fosbury. Perhaps his origins saw to that. But, the same certainly cannot be said of Oldfield. Oldfield was a colossus. He was unique. I was privileged to witness the Woods, Feuerbach, Oldfield pre-competition training circuses in Munich and Oldfield oozed talent, whichever way he chose to throw, and, although the youngest, he was without doubt the star of the show. He chose to use only the conventional O'Brien technique in the competition itself, and finished 6th at 20.91m.

It is easy to imagine what might have happened had Oldfield repeated his inspirational American Trials effort during the Olympic final; yet it couldn't have had more impact than his actions of subsequent years. He made a complete conversion to the rotational method; he stepped away from the mainline sport by becoming professional (that act in itself ensured publicity) and proceeded to throw prodigious distances, including 22.86 meters in 1975. By doing so he exerted a marked influence upon shot putting for many years to come.

So, here we are, almost two decades on, with Fosbury high jump technique in the ascendancy, and rotational shot putting still struggling make significant inroads, except in America and among Scandinavians under strong American educational influence.

The developmental contrast is stark. In 1972, four years after its emergence, the flop technique had influenced high jumping to such an extent that 50% of the best athletes were using it. Four years on from that, the proportion had increased to 80%, and by 1980 only a tiny rump of East German exponents held to the straddle style. In contrast, rotational shot putting had only managed to infiltrate the male sector to a ratio of 1 to 3 by the last Olympic Games. On the women's side we have only witnessed one American exponent of the technique in an Olympic final during the entire period. it has yet to win a major games—hardly a revolution.

While accepting that the technique enjoys pockets of enthusiastic support, it has plainly failed to make great inroads, in Europe in particular. Accepting that the doctrinaire inertia of Communist sporting culture (now becoming apparent as more of our own coaches gain access to this previously closed society) may well have been a limiting influence, one cannot escape the fact that the flop rapidly broke through the barrier, even eventually in East

Germany. Not even the West Germans, for long a strong throwing nation, and certainly not hidebound by the constraints of their eastern brethren, have ever nurtured a top quality "spinner".

Can there be an incipient flaw in the technique?

The claims made of it are summarized in the following four tenets:

1. It increases the range over which the implement can be accelerated.
2. It enables the thrower to assume a more favorable position from which to begin the final putting action.
3. It facilitates superior leg lift at the front of the ring.
4. It brings improved performance to certain throwers.

Subsequent experience and evaluation suggest that:

1. The attainment of infinite range brings with it no guarantee of equally infinite end velocity. Limits exist, and in this particular respect they have shown to be:

   1.1 A limit to the velocity which the athlete is capable of accepting and utilizing on reaching the power position (Fig. 1). The threshold for this appears to lie below that attainable using even O'Brien techniques.

FIG. 1: THE POWER POSITION

   1.2 That significant retardations take place during the mid-third of the spiral path which negate the value of much that precedes them. Although it has been demonstrated that there are clear retardations in Baryshnikov's derivative (Fig. 2), modern spinners have overcome this deficiency by being more active in moving around the implement (Fig. 3) and maintaining its forward translation (Fig. 4) at the power position.

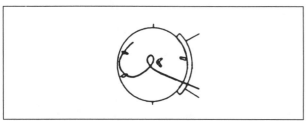

FIG. 2: BARYSHNIKOV'S SPIRAL PATH (J.G. HAY)

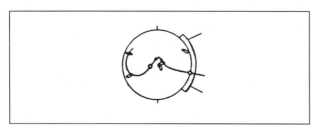

FIG. 3: LAUT'S SPIRAL PATH (J.G. HAY)

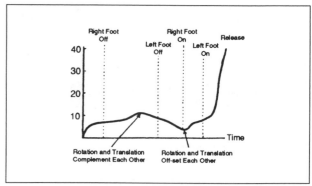

FIG. 4: ROTATIONAL SHOT VELOCITIES (R. GEESE)

2. Herein rests the main potential of the technique. Better rhythmic qualities facilitate the generation of greater torque, and the storage of more kinetic energy from the preceding actions—the result of being able to move the hip axis ahead of the shoulder axis.

   2.1 The technique makes it possible for the shot putter to tap into the benefits of a three-plane system in the way that discus throwers or hammer throwers do. The principle of "hip-lead" or "separation" or "crossing-the-x" (Fig. 5) becomes a more dynamic activity. Feuerbach attempted to utilize this principle. His concepts of "pre-tension" or "open hips" sought separation of the hip and shoulder axes and hip lead. He was limited by the essential two-plane system within which he worked.

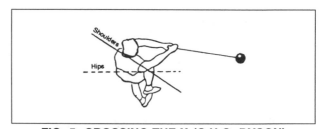

FIG. 5: CROSSING-THE-X (G.H.G. DYSON)

   2.2 The movement of the lower girdle ahead of the upper girdle possesses the added advantage of loading the trunk musculature so that the principle of stretch reflex is evoked when it is eventually brought into play.

   2.3 Entry to an open kinetic link in the transverse plane and to the greater sequential accumulatiuons which can accrue from it (Fig. 6) is entirely dependent upon very fine timing. Because the implement remains close to the axis of rotation, the number of segments involved, and thus the advantages gained, can never match those of the discus or hammer.

3. The restricted dimensions of the 2.135-meter circle forces the rotational shot putter into a power position having a narrower base than either the discus circle or the

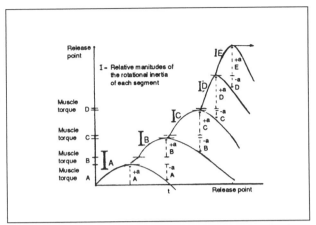

FIG. 6: SEQUENTIAL ACCUMULATIONS OF THE OPEN KINETIC LINK (KREIGHBAUM & BARTHELS)

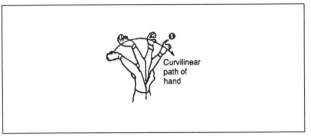

FIG. 7: A CURVILINEAR RELEASE (IN THE SAGGITAL PLANE) (KREIGHBAUM & BARTHELS)

FIG. 8: A RECTILINEAR RELEASE (KREIGHBAUM & BARTHELS)

O'Brien shift permits. This is claimed to facilitate an advantageous double leg shift. It is also claimed therefore that it is suited particularly to men and to those who are especially strong in the legs.

4. Two particular groups are singled out as natural beneficiaries of the technique:

4.1 Those of modest stature and strength.

4.2 Those whose development has stagnated as linear throwers.

The first would suggest a strong reason why women as a group ought to be able to benefit from a change to the rotational style, and since women are relatively stronger in the lower limbs than they are in the upper limbs the preceding tenet ought to reinforce the strength application advantages of such a change. Evidence is that athletes and coaches have declined to apply this principle.

Since the technique is a modification of one originally conceived for a 2.5m circle it is understandable why smaller athletes find it easier to adapt to the confines of the 2.135m one. Does this also indicate that the technique is not really suitable for tall long-limbed athletes (like Baryshnikov who was 1.99m tall)?

A very old adage suggests that "a change is as good as a rest." Perhaps it is just the act of changing, bringing new enthusiasms, which brings about improvements (a technical placebo effect).

Against this must be weighed the length of time that it takes to really master the new style—as reported by many top exponents. Detractors argue that had the same amount of time and effort been channeled into sorting out the problems of the O'Brien technique, similar progress could have been made. What price motivation? What value motivation?

Measured against the claimed advantages rests the fact that one of the final segments of the sequential buildup

(that initiating release) is essentially curvilinear (Fig. 7) in the transverse plane (a pulling action). In the conventional O'Brien form it is rectilinear (Fig. 8) in the saggital plane (a pushing action). The main muscle groups involved are large muscles (legs and torso) and thus not attuned to discrete actions. Timing release is much more of a lottery than it is in the discus or javelin (other examples of curvilinear releases).

It is possible that the kinetic chain is not long enough for the proprioceptive mechanisms involved; that the rotational shot putter is having to use a short, rigid fishing rod, as opposed to the long flexible one available to his discus or hammer counterparts.

Finally, notice must be taken of the fact that all current rotational putters are converted linear throwers. They have thus spent a large part of their lives developing skills which they then had to discard or override. How many inhibitions to the learning process had to be overcome? We can truly access the value of the technique when exponents enter the lists whose only shot put experiences have been rotational ones. Where are the coaches who are going to be brave enough to tread such a path?

Conversely, the principles of motor learning indicate that early motor training ought to be as broad and varied as possible and that later capacities to learn complex skills are heightened by such experience. It thus follows that varied experiences of turning activities and of throwing rotationally could be usefully included in the early movement program of young throwers, indeed of all children. Ten-Step and Sports Hall throwing should not be restricted to linear forms of throwing (i.e., to the overhead throw or shot put) to the exclusion of other forms, as they currently are.

USING THE DYNAMIC START IN THE GLIDE

by Larry Judge, USA

Judge, who is now Assistant Track & Field Coach at the University of South Carolina (formerly at Indiana State), details his approach to the glide technique and offers related drills to help develop the thrower.

Throwing the shot using the linear technique (glide) may be the simplest of all throwing techniques. Movements are confined to a small area and there are no aerodynamic factors involved. However, mastering this rather simple maneuver often takes years, especially if the athlete's initial attempts are left to chance, and bad habits must be corrected.

The rotational technique is more complex but seems to be more easily mastered by the athlete who is comfortable with the discus. The "spin" is said to allow the athlete to generate more speed than the glide.

The major drawback of the rotational technique is that it is inconsistent in achieving a good power position. The challenge facing coaches today is how to combine the speed and range of the spin with the consistent power position of the glide.

In the glide technique used here at Indiana State University, we have combined the best factors of each style to produce the dynamic start in the glide. In this technique the athlete starts in an erect position and initiates the throw aggressively by dropping from the upright position into the glide. This type of start allows the athlete to gain the extra momentum and range he would get with the spin and still have the consistent power position of a glide. Putters who use this technique can achieve superior results even though their basic strength and size may not be as great as other putters.

This article will discuss the approach to the glide technique that was instrumental in transforming Christy Barrett from a 13.00m shot putter to a 16.80m shot putter in three years. Discussion of technique is followed by an explanation of the drills used at Indiana State University.

Success in the shot put is a combination of several factors.

1. **Strength**
   This is acquired through an extensive year-round training program. Consistency is the key.
2. **Technique**
   This is acquired through a complete learning and understanding of proper technique along with continued practice of the proper movements. Timing is more difficult to teach but generally comes as a result of thousands of throws. The coach must set the "model" for the athlete.
3. **Speed or Quickness**
   These factors are largely inherited but are also closely related to strength. Development can be enhanced through explosive exercises along with sprinting all-out for short distances.
4. **Agility**
   Because of the precise footwork and upper body coordination required in the shot the development of agility is extremely important.
5. **Size**
   Size becomes more of a factor on the college level. There is generally a strong correlation between absolute strength and body size.

DISCUSSION OF TECHNIQUE

The body is in the upright position with the left leg parallel and one inch behind the right. The shot is held medium high on the fingers. The number of fingers behind the shot (three or four) is a matter of personal preference. The shot is placed against the neck with the thumb down and the elbow up. Make sure the arm carriage is in a position in which the athlete can give a clean arm strike in the release. Center of gravity is over the support foot, with the torso low, nearly parallel to the ground. The angle of the support leg is near 120 degrees. Focus the eyes at a point six to eight feet away outside the back of the circle and slightly to the right. Make sure the athlete keeps his head up.

THE GLIDE

Movement is initiated by an aggressive drop from the up position settling the hips toward the front of the circle. In the drop the athlete tries to extend the shot outside the back of the ring before driving to the center. This will give the athlete some extra range and will vary from athlete to athlete. Then weight shifts back on support leg heel. The shoulders, eyes, and head remain in starting position.

The free leg drives toward the toe board staying close to the ground. The support foot lands in the center of the ring at a 90° angle.

At Indiana State, the dynamic start is emphasized. The athlete starts in an erect position and actively drops into the glide and moves across the ring. This type of start allows the athlete to build extra momentum and gives the glider the type of momentum a spinner achieves.

An athlete can gain one or two extra feet out of the back of the ring with a smooth dynamic start. This type of start allows the glider to achieve superior results without a great amount of size and strength.

The conventional "T" start requires a great deal of leg power and body mass to create enough force needed for a smooth glide. The majority of athletes at the high school and collegiate level don't have the physical attributes to effectively use the "T" start.

GLIDE

Momentum is produced in the glide as a result of a summation of three distinct movements.

1. Shift the weight
   a. The athlete drops into the glide from the upright position.
   b. This may be felt as falling to the rear
   c. The COG must pass behind the heel before any other movement is initiated.
   d. This movement helps to keep the hips low throughout the glide.

2. Drive front (left) leg for board
   a. The left leg is driven low and directly for the toe board.
   b . The feet should land simultaneously.
   c. This results in a transfer of momentum from the leg to the total body.
   d. The foot should be planted close to the toe board a few inches to the left of the center.
   e. The heel of the left foot is down in the power position.

3. Push-pull with back (right) leg
   a. The right leg executes a rigorous push from the back of the ring, then is immediately pulled under the body and turned as close to 90 degrees as possible.
   b. Almost all weight should land on the ball of the right foot with little, if any, weight on the heel.
   c. The left leg is firm in the power position in order to keep the weight back over the right.

ADDITIONAL COMMENTS

1. Both feet should land simultaneously.
2. Both knees will straighten while executing the glide but should be bent slightly upon landing.
3. The left leg should be kept firm to help keep the right side back.
4. Turning of the feet should begin to open hips in the direction of the throw.
5. Shoulders must be kept closed.
6. "Cross the X" (produces torque position).
7. Left arm hangs like a rope. Hang across body to hold left shoulder closed.
8. Shot is held at base of fingers.
9. Fingers point toward midline (elbow is up).
10. The athlete should concentrate on an early "hit" in the middle of the ring.

DRILLS

Dynamic Glides: Athlete works on the dynamic start by working an aggressive drop into the start.

Phantom Glides: Shadow glides on the track. Do five consecutive glides working on consistency.

Glides with Partner: Partner holds the left hand to keep shoulders closed.

Glides with Crossbar: Use a javelin or bar—work on keeping shoulders closed.

Stop Drill: Glide and stop and perform a standing throw working on the power position and the block.

Three Consecutive Hops: Three consecutive glides without putting the left leg down.

Glides with Object in Middle of Ring: Athlete is forced to pull right foot over object.

Mini-Glide Drill: Athlete performs short glides working on a simultaneous landing of both feet in the power position.

POWER POSITION

From this position at the end of the glide, the drive leg touches down to left side of the toe board and the throw is initiated by the left leg. The throw is initiated by the turning of the support leg foot toward the front of the ring, then the knee and then the hips.

As the lower extremities are driving toward the toe board, the center of gravity is moving forward. The free arm goes long to help slow the rotation of the upper body. The throwing arm and shoulders stay back. The action is a rotate-and-lift-type movement.

THROW

In the full throw, this portion of the movement begins as the glide ends. This is also the position from which we execute our "standing throws."

JUDGE'S PUPIL CHRISTY BARRETT IMPROVED TO A 16.80 SHOT PUTTER USING THE REGIMEN IN THIS ARTICLE.

COMMENTS

1. Heel of back (right) foot must be up so foot can rotate.
2. Drive right knee in direction of throw (rotate hips).
3. Straighten back leg (keeps shot back).
4. Resist with front leg (lifts hips).
5. Rotate hips up and out into throw while keeping shoulders back (torque).
6. Shoulders will follow hips.
7. Strive for "C" position.
8. Left arm—
   a. Drive around with hand wide. Don't exaggerate high low path.
   b. Shorten lever near end of swing (elbow lead). This causes sudden increase in velocity or "pop."
9. Right arm—
   a. Fingers continue to point toward mid-line throughout movement.
   b. Follow-through is to the right, out and down.

POWER POSITION DRILLS

Hip Pops: Athlete pops hip keeping upper body back. Can be done with or without a shot.

Hip Pops with Partner: Partner holds left arm while athlete pops hip.

Hip Pops with Bar: Athlete performs a hip pop with a bar or broom stick on his back emphasizing hips only.

Glide and Pop: Athlete glides and pops hips.

Standing Throw #1: Athlete rotates hips and throws shot with a tilted axis. Emphasis is on hip rotation and there is no forward thrust.

Standing Throw #2: Athlete drives upper body all the way through. Emphasis is on the one (hip rotation), two (shoulder rotation) action.

Step-Over Stands: Athlete does a standing throw with no reverse and steps over the toe board working on his follow through.

PUT

The forward rotation of the support leg creates an upward lift of the hips. The shoulders rotate (slowed by long free arm). As the transfer of power occurs the shot is accelerated quickly. The elbow remains up as the shot is pushed away from the body with the thumb down. Remind throwers, the action is "hips up and arm out."

At the end of the release, there is a finger/wrist snap. In the glide the athlete should concentrate on hitting the throw early, before the hips drift forward. The emphasis should be on an aggressive "hit" in the middle of the ring. The thrower should strive to get into the power position as early as possible.

FOLLOW-THROUGH

The arm follows through after the release. The rotational force caused by the arm follow-through should be followed by the head and shoulders. The putting arm is driven out and the power leg is thrown toward the left sector. The feet switch position. If the athlete watches the shot, the rotational forces are interrupted and transferred out over the toe board, causing a foul. Always have athletes stay in during practice.

REVERSE

The reverse is used to dissipate momentum at the front of the ring and to prevent fouling. The reverse is the result of a good hip drive and should not be forced. At Indiana State the reverse is performed on only the final ten glides or spins. The no-reverse is used to set up the hip drive and block. The reverse is never performed on stand-

Order of Drills	Collegiate Women	Collegiate Men	High School Boys	High School Girls
Wrist Flips	12# (3)	20# (3)	16# (3)	12# (3)
Front Push	12# (3)	20# (3)	16# (3)	12# (3)
Standing Throws #1	12# (5)	20# (5)	16# (5)	12# (5)
(No reverse) #2	12# (8)	20# (8)	16# (8)	12# (3)
Glides (no reverse)	12# (5) 10# (6) 4K (5)	20# (5) 18# (6) 16# (5)	16# (5) 14# (6) 12# (5)	12# (5) 10# (6) 4K (5)
Glides (with reverse)	4K (10) or (15)	16# (10) (15)	12# (10) or (15)	4K (10) or (15)

ing throws. The standing throw is used to set up the hip drive and is merely a check point for the technique.

COMMENTS

1. Reverse should not begin before release.
2. Allow momentum to carry into circular path, not straight out over the toe board.
3. Lower hips for stability.
4. Do not attempt to follow shot with eyes.
5. Do not rehearse fouling in practice.
6. Teach athletes a late reverse.

THROWING DRILL PROGRESSION (GLIDE)

1. **Wrist Flip:** Work on keeping elbow up and getting a flip off the fingers (warm up wrist).
2. **Front Push:** A wrist flip done with the right leg back and emphasis on right-side speed.
3. **Standing Throw #1:** Work on rotating hips while keeping upper body back.
4. **Standing Throw #2 (no reverse):** Start from an upright (stickman) position with the hips over the leg. Bend a little more and use warmup. Work only for positions and one-two action.
5. **Glide (no reverse):** The majority of the practice is done without the reverse to insure proper hip drive and the block.
6. **Glide (full technique):** These are done at the end of a workout when the nerves are ready and positions are right.

OVERLOAD TRAINING

The best way to achieve a strong, snappy throw with the dynamic glide is to use the overload principle in the daily throwing regimen. For an athlete to perform effectively the competition implement must feel light. In early to mid-season training, the emphasis is on a lot of work with heavy implements to build throwing strength or power. This type of training with heavy shots is the key to success with the dynamic glide. A ladder type system is employed, starting heavy and moving to a lighter implement as the athlete fatigues and technique deteriorates. The object of this is to make the competition implement feel light.

This type of workout helps improve power and will help the athlete make up for deficiencies in the weight room. Six weeks of this will bring immediate results.

As the season progresses the ladder can be adjusted downward for more speed work. The table above shows a typical workout for a collegiate or prep thrower using the overload system of throwing.

CONCLUSION

In training shot putters at Indiana State University, the philosophy is to make the athlete feel as strong and explosive as possible with the implement. Technically, the dynamic start is employed in the glide to give the athlete some extra momentum out of the back of the circle. Training-wise, besides working hard in the weight room, overload is achieved by throwing with heavy implements to build specific "throwing strength."

In the short time available to prepare for competition the training must be "specific." Many coaches disagree with this philosophy, and feel athletes should train light and work for speed. Speed training is definitely part of the training regimen. But, by throwing heavy and making the jumps in implements the athlete feels fast with the competitive implement.

Using a system of overload is the quickest way to make a weak athlete feel strong with the competitive implement and the bottom line is it brings results fast. After all, the object is to make the competitive implement feel light on the day of the competition.

VARIATIONS IN SHOT PUT METHODS AND THEIR APPLICATION

by Bill Larsen, Australia

The author looks at the different shot put variations and comes to the conclusion that the advantages gained by one method over another are more often than not compensated for by disadvantages in another aspect.

It has yet to be convincingly demonstrated that any single method of shot put technique even in general terms is clearly superior. This together with differing physical characteristics and the specific requirements of groups—such as decathletes, heptathletes and young athletes—is ensuring that the different techniques continue to thrive side by side. It is therefore important that coaches fully understand, not only the advantages and disadvantages of each method, but also the relative suitability of each method for a particular athlete.

EVALUATION OF TECHNIQUES

The major points of evaluation in a comparative analysis of shot put technique are:

- The initial velocity generated by the shift or turn.

- The efficiency of the transition to the delivery phase.

- The range of movement of the shot and the amount of torque generated.

- The stability of the delivery position and the rate of acceleration in the delivery phase.

It would be virtually impossible to find a single method which produces the highest return in all of these points and, in reality, we have to trade off losses in one area against gains in another.

While there has been a plethora of minor and often idiosyncratic variations of shot put method over the years, competition throwing still reflects three major points of divergence: the O'Brien shift versus the discus turn, the short-shift-long-base versus the long-shift-short-base, and the single-support braced delivery versus the double-support.

Each of these methods needs to be evaluated, not only in terms of the general requirements of the event, but also in relation to the needs of specific groups and types of throwers.

The Glide

The shift, or glide, has been with us in one variation or another since Parry O'Brien literally turned his back on the throwing circle in the early 1950s. The method has a lot going for it. Its explosive delivery phase allows for an extremely high rate of acceleration, it generates torque and, in spite of the reversed starting position, maintains the shot movement in a relatively straight line.

Furthermore, it incorporates positional characteristics that allow for a relatively smooth transition from glide to delivery and the maintenance of stability, both in the center of the circle and during the delivery.

It also has another very useful advantage. It is easily broken down into logical and clearly defined parts for demonstration and practice.

However, the method has its drawbacks, most of them occurring in the back of the circle. Because of the reversed starting position, the initial velocity generated by the glide is not high (1.4 to 2.8 m/sec), there is a clear break in the center of the circle where loss of velocity occurs, and both the length of the shot path and the amount of torque are limited.

Also, the initial movement can be complex, requiring almost simultaneous but different movements from the legs, and it is difficult for beginning throwers to coordinate. This last problem is serious enough to result in the teaching of a useful, but not entirely satisfactory, intermediate method of traversing the circle—namely the "step-back."

The Rotational Method

The relative stagnation of the shot put World record between 1967 and 1983 led to a heightened interest in the discus turn or rotational method of putting. Although this situation has changed somewhat, thanks to the efforts of Timmermann and a rejuvenated Beyer, the rotational method remains a viable alternative.

The suitability of the discus turn for adaptation to the shot is partly limited by two factors over which the thrower has no control: a smaller circle and the rules of the event which prevent the implement from gaining additional velocity from a wide turning radius.

In contrast to the shift, however, the rotation still produces a high initial (angular) velocity and, when the legs are driven well ahead of the upper body, creates impressive torque. The one and a half turns result in the shot being accelerated over a longer path, which promises a higher release velocity.

The method also has other advantages. In contrast to the shift, most of the rotational problems are concentrated at the front of the circle.

If the transition from shift to delivery is smooth because of the ability to vary the length of the glide, that of the rotation certainly is not. For a rotational shot putter to put in an effective block is difficult and requires considerable strength.

This makes it hard for the thrower to deliver the implement without either overbalancing or dissipating part of the force away from the direction of the throw.

Also, because the delivery position of the rotational shot putter tends to be more forward—that is, has less "lean back" than the shift—the shot moves over a shorter vertical range during the strike, thus requiring the use of a wider throwing base.

Variation in the method of delivery provides a major point of divergence for shot putters, particularly for those using a modified O'Brien shift. The two distinct approaches that have evolved are characterized by single- and double-leg support in the delivery phase. There are, of course, throwers who use combinations of some features of both methods.

Single-Leg Support

The single-support system is distinguished by an upper body action similar to that employed by javelin throwers. The sequence of clockwork-like movements is right knee, right hip, left knee and right elbow. It climaxes with a firmly braced left leg, which provides a stable delivery platform and utilizes the torque generated by the shift and subsequent hip rotation to produce a powerful delivery.

Following Newton's Third Law of Motion, the reverse occurs late, thus making full use of the force applied through the leg to the ground.

When performed correctly, this method has considerable potential for gains in the rate of acceleration. However, in addition to the limitations imposed by a single-support delivery, it is extremely hard to perform correctly.

Double-Leg Support

On the surface, the alternate method appears more straightforward, relying more on the concentration of effort on one powerful, double-legged lunge from a low squat position than on the sequential links of the single-support system.

However, the preparation for the elongated lunge action is also complex. It begins with a sideways drift of the hips over the left leg and an extension of the left leg, followed, in order, by movement from the right knee, left knee, right hip and right elbow. Its obvious appeal lies in the use of both legs in a powerful delivery, an action which utilizes specific power gains from the squat lift.

It also avoids some of the timing and coordination problems of the other method. The most common faults of throwers using this type of delivery are a tendency to lift the hips rather than push them with a strong downward action of the right leg and a failure to obtain the lower center ring position, demanded for efficient use of a double-support delivery. Gains in lift also tend to be partially offset by a less linear delivery.

Some of the common delivery faults can be traced to combinations of inappropriate features of the two methods. For example, the bracing of the left leg, which is essential for the single-support delivery, is contradictory to the double-support action.

Even Grigalka's suggested combination of a vigorous trunk rotation from a low position is negated in very the same article in which he introduces the idea when he points out the need for a relatively high position in forming a strong base for efficient trunk movement.

Whatever method is used, a clear understanding of the principles of both methods is required to avoid the use of combinations that are incompatible.

Orthodox and East German Shifts

There are also two distinct schools of thought when it comes to the nature of the shift itself: the orthodox method, using a long shift to the center of the circle with the resultant short delivery base, and the East German method, with its short shift and consequent long delivery base.

A long shift makes it comparatively easy to obtain a powerful "leg under" position and enables the thrower to remain low. However, the length of the shot path in the delivery phase is reduced and the transition is awkward.

By comparison, the short shift produces a long acceleration path and relatively smooth transition, but the center ring position is higher and the legs wide apart. For all but super strong throwers this results in a difficult delivery position.

On balance, a long shift would appear to be more compatible with a double-support delivery and a short shift with a single-support delivery.

The continued survival of such technically different shot put methods is due, primarily, to a lack of certainty regarding their relative efficiency. There is another reason, of course. Shot putters are not a race of clones. They differ in age, sex, height, weight, strength, speed and degree of coordination. They differ also in the orientation of their shot put activities, from specialist senior putters to decathletes, heptathletes and young throwers still actively engaged in more than one throwing event.

MULTIPLE EVENTS

Because the decathlete has to prepare for 10 events and the heptathlete for seven, the time available for shot put preparation is limited, and the training pressure on an athlete's energy reserves is quite severe. For these reasons, any method which allows a transfer of technique and/or specific conditioning between events has some obvious value.

It would therefore appear logical for a decathlete to adopt a rotational style of shot putting to gain maximum advantage from his discus preparation. However, it can be argued that essential differences in the two turns, not to mention the difference in the size of the throwing circles, will result in some interference in both events. In practice, coaches have found that it is both difficult to learn and very risky in a three-throw competition.

A second problem with multiple event throwers is that the physical requirements of the component events are such as to necessitate a significantly different physical profile from that of specialist shot putter. Because considerable strength is required in the delivery phase of the rotation, it seems the use of this method by decathletes is argued against.

For the same reason, multiple event athletes generally appear physically more suited to a long shift than a short shift. Similarly, because they are relatively light and because their range of hurdling, jumping and throwing events assumes a high degree of coordination, a single-support delivery would be more appropriate than one employing double-support.

YOUNG ATHLETES

Coaches working with younger athletes also have a set of requirements largely peculiar to their situation. The relevant factors are strength level, skill acquisition and learning problems and event selection. Each of these factors can play an important part in the choice of method.

The young thrower, particularly the beginner, does not have serious ingrained faults nor a long-term addiction to one way of throwing.

Although theoretically, a free choice of method would therefore appear possible, in reality the choice is limited. For a start, the beginner cannot consider great strength as an option in the short- or even mid-term. Consequently, the use by beginners of methods requiring relatively high levels of strength can lead to compensatory modifications in movement resulting in long-term technique faults. This means, for example, that the short-shift-long-base variation would usually be regarded as unsuitable.

When it comes to decisions on how to go about teaching the shot put to beginners, the conventional wisdom favors two alternatives. In one of these, because the standing put accounts for approximately 90% of the final result, the athlete is first taught a standing put and persists with this alone for some time, before being introduced to a modified O'Brien shift. The other approach favors the introduction of an intermediate link, the step-back, before proceeding to the shift.

The argument in favor of an intermediate stage is that the step-back is easier to learn than the shift, leads smoothly into the delivery phase and provides immediate returns to learners, while they strive to reach a level of development where the shift can be successfully introduced. The obvious argument against it is that the two movements are essentially different, even to the point of being initiated from opposite legs.

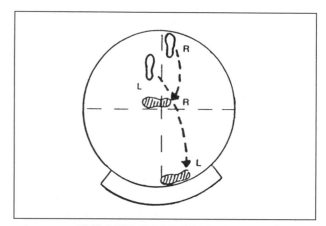

**THE STEP-BACK TECHNIQUE
RECOMMENDED ONLY FOR YOUNG ATHLETES
IN GROUP TEACHING SITUATIONS**

For this reason it appears reasonable to advocate the use of the step-back in schools and beginners clinics where athletes with varying levels of commitment are being instructed in a group situation. On the other hand, when an athlete comes to a coach with the single idea of becoming a shot putter or multiple event athlete, it would be advisable to begin, as soon as possible, the difficult task of developing an efficient shift.

CONCLUSIONS

It is possible to draw some reasonably safe conclusions. It is clear that a range of significantly different shot put variations remains valid. In general, it can be stated that the advantages gained by one method over another in one aspect of the throw are more often than not compensated for by disadvantages in another aspect. Further, characteristics can be identified within each shot put variation that make it particularly suited for application with specific sub-groups of throwers.

PRE-SEASON PREPARATION FOR THE COLLEGIATE SHOT PUTTER

by Larry Judge, USA

An optimal performance in the shot put is the result of a carefully planned program that integrates several components of training. Judge is currently Assistant Track & Field Coach at the University of South Carolina. He was an assistant coach at Indiana State University when he wrote this article.

Shot putters must acquire great strength, power, agility, flexibility and skill to be successful. While throwing the shot is the simplest of all throwing techniques, mastering this maneuver takes years of preparation.

An optimal performance in the shot put is the result of a carefully planned program integrating several components of training, including aspects of Olympic lifting, power lifting and bodybuilding, as well as running, jumping and throwing. Improvement often comes from careful attention to detail.

This article outlines the approach to pre-season preparation used by Indiana State University (ISU) throwers, including 17.34-meter collegiate shot putter Christy Barrett, who competed at the 1991 World University Games.

Track & field is unique when compared to other sports because the season is geared toward peaking for three or four important meets. This makes periodization of the training program essential. A shot putter's calendar year is broken into the following training phases:

- the pre-season conditioning program from September through November;

- the strength-power phase in October and December;

- a peaking and maintenance phase in January and February, with the indoor season climaxing at the end of February and the beginning of March;

- a repetition of the strength-power phase from mid-March through April;

- peaking and maintenance again in May and June to prepare for outdoor conference and national championships.

The months of July and August are considered the active rest or transition phase in preparation for fall.

FALL PREPARATION PHASE

The primary objective of the fall preparation program is to ensure peak performance in key competitions. ISU throwers are trained as complete athletes and this is reflected in their practice regimen. To understand the pre-season program at ISU, different training phases must be understood. Our pre-season conditioning program assumes that the athletes will return with fitness levels ranging from sedentary to fairly active. At Indiana State, the year begins with low intensity and high volume to prepare the athletes for more specific, higher intensity work.

Each training session is designed to fit into a one-week microcycle. A group of three to four microcycles forms a mesocycle. Each mesocycle is designed to build on the previous one, and three to four mesocycles fit in the macrocycle. At ISU, two macrocycles form the annual plan. The first macrocycle extends through the indoor season and the second extends through the outdoor nationals. The pre-season program is similar to those for the other field events but has less emphasis on aerobic activity and more emphasis on strength and technique development. The physical components periodized for the year include strength training, medicine ball throws, running, plyometrics, circuits and shot put throws.

STRENGTH-POWER PHASE

The strength-power phase begins in November and is very demanding. In this phase, quantity is reduced and quality is increased. For many of the throwing drills, the regulation shot is replaced by an overweight implement to build strength. The intensity of the medicine ball and plyometric exercises are increased, repetitions are lowered and the number of exercises is decreased. The emphasis is on all-out strength and power development.

PEAKING AND MAINTENANCE PHASE

An in-season peaking phase is the same for the indoor and outdoor seasons. There is a mini-peak at the end of each week with the major peak at the end of the phase. A typical week consists of heavy throwing and weight lifting early in the week, with low repetitions (3-5), basic exercises (bench, squat, clean) at high intensity (80-90% of 1-rep maximum [1RM]).

During the early indoor and outdoor seasons, emphasis is on strength development. The middle of the week consists of light lifting, used for nerve stimulation, and light throwing. The end of the week is used for rest.

Close to the important competitions the work load is decreased. Two weeks prior to an important competition, heavy squats are discontinued and the lifting and throwing is light and fast.

MINI-TRANSITION PHASE

Between the indoor and outdoor seasons, a three- to four-week strength-power stage is used to rebuild the base. This is also referred to as a mini-transition phase that is used to facilitate physiological and psychological restoration. The lifting and training volumes are increased and intensity is decreased. Medicine ball exercises, plyometrics and a general strength circuit are performed bi-weekly. The athlete is then ready to enter the in-season peaking phase for the outdoor season.

THE PRE-SEASON PROGRAM

In the fall, the development of strength and endurance specific to throwing is emphasized. Pre-season weight lifting is considered a hypertrophy or bodybuilding stage. The emphasis is on building an endurance base in the weightroom for future heavy lifting. Repetitions should be high (8-10), but the athletes should be encouraged to increase repetition maximums.

Workouts are based on a percentage of repetition maximums. Eight sets per body part are performed with two to three minutes rest between sets. Lifting is suggested four to six days per week with each body part worked bi-weekly.

Throwers also need to perform general conditioning activities that improve strength and coordination through bodyweight activities. General conditioning for throwers improves overall fitness and should remain fairly specific to anaerobic activities. Aerobic conditioning will not be emphasized but will include an 800-meter warmup run, a general strength circuit done bi-weekly, a jump rope circuit, and an 800-meter cooldown.

Each workout should include a partner flexibility routine, form-running drills and abdominal exercises to enhance postural strength. A general strength circuit—

consisting of five bodyweight exercises performed twice a week—plus medicne ball exercises and plyometrics are performed on days opposite the general strength circuit. Long sprints (150-200 meters) are done twice a week and short sprints (30-100 meters) are done on opposite days.

Pre-season throwing includes repetitive activity designed to establish patterns and pathways to work from. Drills are employed in each of the throwing events, stressing proper body positions. Each throw can be broken down into parts and each part drilled either empty-handed or with an implement. This is an excellent time of year to teach the proper model to athletes so they can work on proper technique and change bad habits. The following is an example of a one-week microcycle:

Monday.
Warmup, flexibility, form drills, plyometrics, technique, long sprints, weights, cooldown.

Tuesday.
Warmup, flexibility, strength circuit, technique, medicine ball, short sprints, weights, cooldown.

Wednesday.
Warmup, flexibility, jump rope circuit, individual technique work, weights, cooldown.

Thursday.
Warmup, flexibility, strength circuit, technique, medicine ball, short sprints, weights, cooldown.

Friday.
Warmup, flexibility, form drills, plyometrics, technique, long sprints, weights, cooldown.

Saturday.
Warmup, flexibility, weights.

Sunday.
10- to 15-minute easy run.

Each component of the pre-season program is explained in detail in the following section, followed by an example of how each aspect can be integrated into the program.

WARMUP

Steady running for five to 10 minutes followed by flexibility, form running and acceleration runs should be an integral part of the pre-season preparation phase. At ISU, 3-5 sets of abdominals are performed daily as part of the warmup.

The 800-meter warmup and cooldown run, the strength circuit and high-repetition weight lifting will help build pre-season endurance. Endurance specific to throwers is needed to prevent muscular fatigue, which can inhibit motor learning during lengthy training sessions.

As more intense preparation and competition phases follow, some elements of the warmup can be reduced to two days per week. The warmup and cooldown runs should continue throughout the season.

FLEXIBILITY

Stretching must be incorporated into training as part of the warmup and should follow light jogging. This aspect of training is essential for athletes, as it allows full freedom of movement about all joints and enhances muscle elasticity. Flexibility should be done with a partner. Gradual "stretch and hold" methods should be used to elongate the elastic elements. Stretching should also be done after each training session to take advantage of muscle spindle fatigue, prevent soreness and enhance muscle tendon elasticity.

GENERAL STRENGTH CIRCUIT

The general strength circuit consists of bodyweight exercises grouped to form a circuit to stress the aerobic system, build strength and enhance coordination and body awareness.

Athletes must be able to move their bodyweight efficiently. Often, athletes have trouble manipulating their bodyweight because they limit their training to free weights. The general strength circuit causes neuromuscular adaptations that improve coordination and body awareness.

The exercises in the strength circuit include pushups, clap pushups, crunches, leg tosses, leg scissors, chinups,

---

TABLE 1. PRE-SEASON CONDITIONING EXERCISES

Warmup
Jog 800 meters, partner-up and prepare to do the flexibility routine with a partner.

Flexibility
All stretching performed with a partner.

The stretches should be held 10-15 seconds and performed slowly and statically. Recommended stretches include:

1. Loosen upper body—rotate arms, rotate neck, rotate trunk and perform five reps each way.

2. Partner tricep stretch—you hold arm behind head, partner pulls down on wrist.

3. Standing pectoral stretch—hold arms extended behind back and partner will pull them together.

4. Shoulder and pectoral stretch—clasp hands behind head and have partner pull back on your elbows.

5. Hip stretch—sit down on the ground with one leg extended and the other crossed over it, looking over the opposite shoulder.

6. Lower back stretch—lie on your back with legs extended, then cross one extended leg over the other at a 90° angle. Have a partner help you hold.

7. Hamstring stretch—lie on back with legs extended, have partner pull leg back toward your head. Repeat each leg three times, trying for improvement.

8. Standing quad stretch—stand balancing against a fence on one leg and grasp the other leg by the ankle.

9. Calf stretch—stand leaning against a fence with both hands, one leg extended behind and other one bent providing pressure.

General Strength Circuit
1. Crunches x 30
2. Clap pushups x 10
3. Leg toss x 20
4. Pushups x 15
5. V-ups x 20
6. Leg scissors x 20 in and out x 20

Medicine Ball (10 repetitions of each)
Catch and throw
Partner pass
Overhead throw on knees
Twists
Situps
Shot flips on knees
Shot drops
Overhead explosions

Plyometrics
5 x 5 boxes (double leg hop)
3 x 5 rotational boxes (sides, 180° 360°)
5 x depth jumps
5 x hurdle hops
5 x broad jumps

Jump Rope Exercises
1. 30 sec warmup: regular jump
2. Jump rope circuit 15 sec each: regular jump, side to side, front to back, double jump, skipping
3. 30 sec cool down: regular jump

Sprints
An example of a microcycle for sprints during pre-season preparation:

Monday	long sprints
Tuesday	short sprints
Wednesday	off
Thursday	short sprints
Friday	long sprints
Saturday	rest
Sunday	10-15 minute easy run

Short sprints (choose one)	1. 5 x 30 meters
	2. 5 x 60 meters
Medium sprints (choose one)	1. 4 x 80 meters
	2. 4 x 100 meters
Long sprints (choose one)	1. 3 x 150 meters
	2. 3 x 200 meters

TABLE 2. WEIGHT LIFTING—SEPTEMBER HYPERTROPHY PHASE

Monday
Legs
Abdominals (3 sets)
Squats (see percentage)
St. leg deadlift 3 x 8
Leg ext. 3 x 10
Leg curl
Calf raise 3 x 15

Tuesday
Chest and Triceps

Abdominals
Bench (see percentage)
Incline 3 x 10
Pullover 3 x 10
Close grips 3 x 10
Push downs 3 x 10

Wednesday
Back, Shoulders and Biceps

Abdominals
Cleans (see percentage)
Dumbbell military 3 x 8
Chins 3 x 5 (men)
Lat pulls 3 x 10
Dumbbell row 3 x 8
Preacher curl 3 x 8
Dumbbell curl 3 x 8

Thursday
Legs

Abdominals (3 sets)
Squat (see percentage)
Lunges 2 x 10
Leg ext. 3 x 10
Leg curl 3 x 10
Calf ext. 3 x 15

Friday
Chest and Triceps

Abdominals (3 sets)
Bench (see percentage)
Dumbell incline 2 x 10
Flys 3x 10
French curls 3 x 10
Dips 3 x 10

Saturday
Back, Shoulders and Biceps
Abdominals. (3 sets)
Cleans (see percentage)
BNP 10, 8, 6
Lat raise 3 x 8
Chins 3 x 5 (men)
Lat pulls 4 x 8
Cable row 3 x 8
Preacher curls 3 x 12
Dumbbell curls 3 x 10

Percentage for bench and squat (estimate 10 rep max)   Percentage for cleans (estimate 5 rep max)

		Workout 1		Workout 2				Workout 1		Workout 2	
Week	1	5 x 10	75%	4 x 10	85%	Week	1	5 x 5	75%	4 x 5	85%
	2	4 x 10	80%	3 x 10	90%		2	4 x 5	80%	3 x 5	90%
	3	4 x 10	85%	2 X 10	95%		3	4 x 5	85%	2 X 5	95%
	4	4 x 10	80%	1 X 10	100% (try for 10 rep max)		4	4 x 5	80%	1 X 5	100%
	5	Start sets of 5									

OCTOBER STRENGTH/POWER PHASE

Monday
Chest, Shoulders and Triceps

Abdominals (3 sets)
Squats (see percentage)

Front squats 3 x 5
Leg press 10, 8, 6
Calf raise 3 x 15

Tuesday
Legs
Abdominals (3 sets)
Bench (see percentage)

Incline 3 x 5
Close grips 3 x 5
BNP 3 x 5
Push downs 3 x 6

Wednesday
Legs

Abdominals (3 sets)
Cleans (see percentage)
Chins 3 x 5
Lat pulls 5 x 6
Dumbbell rows 3 x 6
Standing curl 3 x 6

Dumbbell curl 3 x 6

Thursday
Legs

Abdominals (3 sets)
Squats (see percentage)
Lunges 2 x 8
Leg ext. 3 x 6
Leg curl 3 x 6
Calf raise 3 x 12

Friday
Chest, Shoulders and Triceps

Abdominals (3 sets)
Bench (see percentage)
Incline 3 x 5
Close grips 3 x 5
Weighted dips 3 x 5
French curls 3 x 8

Saturday
Back and Biceps

Abominals (3 sets)
Cleans (see percentages)
Snatches
Chins 3 x 5
Lat pulls 4 x 8
Bent row 3 x 8
Preacher curl 4 x 8
Dumbbell curl 3 x 8

Percentage for bench and squat (estimate 5 rep max)

Percentage for cleans

		Workout 1		Workout 2				Workout 1		Workout 2	
Week	1	4 x 5	85%	5 x 5	75%						
	2	4 x 5	90%	5 x 5	80%	Week	1	4 x 4	85%	5 x 4	75%
	3	3 x 5	95%	5 X 5	85%		2	4 x 4	90%	5 x 4	80%
	4	1 x 5	100%	4 X 5	70%		3	3 x 4	95%	5 X 4	85%
	5	Start sets of 5					4	1 x 4	100%	4 X 4	70%

back hyperextensions and dips. An example of a suggested pre-season circuit is in Table 1. The number of repetitions for each exercise should start at 20-25 for abdominal exercises and 15-20 for upper-body exercises. These should be adjusted to suit the athlete, and as fitness improves, the athlete should perform more repetitions or repeat the circuit.

MEDICINE BALL

This training consists of a group of exercises performed with a 2-kilogram ball in order to strengthen the abdominals and torso. These exercises help improve flexibility, strength and coordination, and can be valuable in adding an increased load to all muscle groups. These drills are particularly useful for developing ballistic strength in the trunk, back and shoulder girdle. Athletes should pair up and follow the exercises listed in Table 1. Ten repetitions should be performed in each exercise, and as the athletes progress, the number of repetitions should be increased or a heavier ball used.

PLYOMETRICS

One of the objectives in training for power is to involve as many motor units (muscle fibers) as possible in a quick, explosive contraction. Plyometrics involves simultaneous voluntary and involuntary muscle contractions. Therefore, more motor units are called upon during a single contraction of this type than would be used in either contraction alone.

Plyometrics is an eccentric contraction followed immediately by a concentric contraction that helps train the fast-twitch fibers specific to throwing. Plyometrics—including box jumps, depth jumps, hurdle hops and many types of bounding drills—should be performed in moderation only twice a week in the pre-season and once a week during the season. Plyometrics should not be performed by athletes with orthopedic injuries.

STRENGTH TRAINING

Strength is the basis for all other aspects of training. A stronger athlete can perform better technically and achieve higher levels of performance. Strength training must be a major element in the training of a successful thrower and must be carried out with a planned program throughout the year.

The preparation begins with the hypertrophy phase in September (Table 2). This should encompass a wide variety of exercises and involve all muscle groups. These exercises should include the classic power lifts and Olympic lifts, but must also include supplementary or support exercises more specific to throwing events. Alternate light and heavy workouts, and work each body part bi-weekly.

Base each workout on a percentage of a repetition maximum for the particular mesocycle. In September, perform sets of 10 repetitions. In October drop to sets of five repetitions and in November move to sets of eight.

The jump from 10 to five repetitions has proven to be very effective as a means of gaining strength because the sudden decrease in volume and rise in intensity shocks the

TABLE 3. TRAINING FOR THE SHOT PUT (PRE-SEASON)

Collegiate	Collegiate				High School		
Order of Drills	Women		Men		Boys		Girls	
Drill	Wt.	#	Wt.	#	Wt.	#	Wt.	#
Wrist Flips	12 lb	(3)	20 lb	(3)	16 lb	(3)	12 lb	(3)
Front Push	12 lb	(3)	20 lb	(3)	16 lb	(3)	12 lb	(3)
Standing Throws #1	12 lb	(5)	20 lb	(5)	16 lb	(5)	12 lb	(5)
#2	12 lb	(8)	20 lb	(8)	16 lb	(8)	12 lb	(3)
Glides	12 lb	(5)	20 lb	(5)	16 lb	(5)	12 lb	(5)
	10 lb	(6)	18 lb	(6)	14 lb	(6)	10 lb	(6)
	4 kg	(5)	16 lb	(5)	12 lb	(5)	4 kg	(5)
Glides (with reverse)	4 kg	(15)	16 lb	(15)	12 lb	(15)	4 kg	(15)

•All drills are performed without the reverse unless indicated

TRAINING FOR THE SHOT PUT (IN SEASON)

Collegiate	Collegiate				High School		
Order of Drills	Women		Men		Boys		Girls	
Drill	Wt.	#	Wt.	#	Wt.	#	Wt.	#
Standing Throws #1	12 lb	(5)	20 lb	(5)	16 lb	(5)	12 lbb	(5)
#2	12 lb	(6)	20 lb	(6)	16 lb	(6)	12 lb	(6)
Glides	12 lb	(3)	20 lb	(3)	16 lb	(3)	12 lb	(3)
	10 lb	(3)	18 lb	(3)	14 lb	(3)	10 lb	(3)
	4 kg	(3)	15 lb	(3)	12 lb	(3)	4 kg	(3)
Glides (with reverse)	4 kg	(10)	16 lb	(10)	12 lb	(10)	4 kg	(10)
(with reverse)	8 lb	(8)	14 lb	(8)	10 lb	(8)	8 lb	(8)

TABLE 4. EXPLANATION OF THROWING SEQUENCE DRILLS (GLIDE)

Wrist Flip: Stand at the front of the ring with both feet at the toeboard, the shot off the neck and at the shoulder. Flip the shot with the elbow up and the thumb down. Work on keeping elbow up and flipping off the fingers (this drill warms up wrist).

Front Push: Stand at the front of the ring with both feet at the toeboard, the shot off the neck and at the shoulder. Step back with the drive leg and turn the upper body slightly toward the back of the ring. Flip the shot with the elbow up and the thumb down. The front push is done like a wrist flip, but with right leg back and emphasis on right side speed.

Standing Throw #1: Rotate hips and throw the shot with a tilted axis at a 45°+ angle. Emphasis is on hip rotation with no forward thrust. Work for position only and do not reverse. Work on rotating hips while keeping upper body back.

Standing Throw #2: Start from an upright (stickman) position with the hips over the leg. Bend a little more on each throw during warmup. Drive the upper and lower body all the way through. Emphasis is on a 1-2 action: 1. hip rotation and 2. shoulder rotation. Work for position only and do not reverse.

Glide (no reverse): The first 15 or 20 glides are done without the reverse. The majority of the practice is done without the reverse to ensure proper hip drive and the block.

Glide (full technique): These are done at the end of a workout when the nerves are ready and positions are set up by the no-reverse workout. Reverse and work on the rhythm of the full technique.

---

system. This will help promote faster gains in the training intensity of the throwing. Sets of five also prepare the athlete to handle heavier loads for sets of eight in November.

Lifting should be performed six days per week during the summer, September and October; four days per week in November through January; and three days per week during the competitive season.

THROWING OVERWEIGHT IMPLEMENTS

In the pre-season preparation phase, the athlete should work with heavy shots to build throwing strength. This serves as the final ingredient in our fall preparation phase and is the key to success with the dynamic glide. A ladder-type system is used, starting heavy and moving to a lighter implement as the athlete tires and technique deteriorates. This workout helps improve power and makes up for deficiencies in the weightroom.

Six weeks of this will bring immediate results. As the season progresses the ladder can be adjusted downward for more speed work. Table 3 includes a typical throwing workout for a collegiate or prep thrower. The different throwing drills are explained in Table 4.

Using heavy shots can help build specific throwing strength, as well as improve core strength and technique. Often, athletes can muscle lighter shots and get away with bad habits. But when using heavy shots, athletes must concentrate on proper technique to manipulate the overweight implement.

CONCLUSION

Success in throwing events is no accident. An optimal peak performance in the shot put is the result of a carefully planned program integrating several components of training. Training for the shot put includes aspects of Olympic lifting, power lifting, and bodybuilding, as well as running, jumping and throwing. The coach must formulate the proper mix according to the needs of each athlete. For optimal performance, no detail should be left to chance. The incorporation of periodization into the training program of a shot putter is essential. However, consistency is the key to success in any training program.

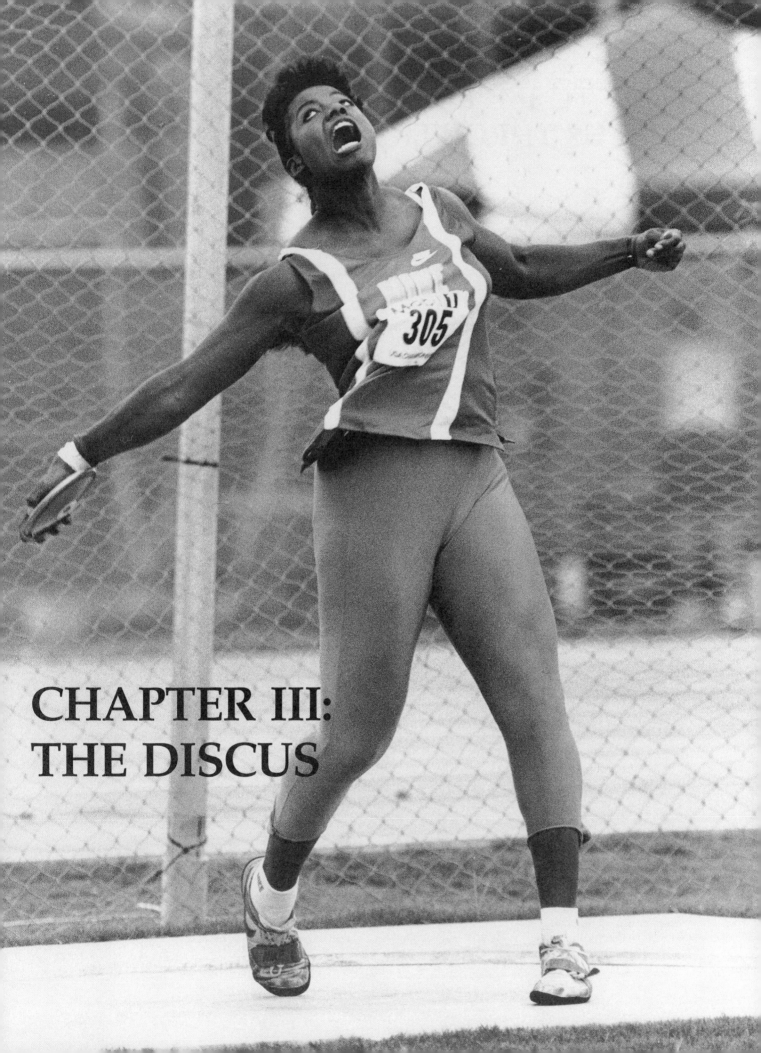

CHAPTER III:
THE DISCUS

HOW TO IMPROVE TALENTED YOUNG DISCUS THROWERS

by Lou Taylor, Australia

A realistic approach to the skill development and conditioning of young discus throwers who have achieved an acceptable performance level and are looking to go beyond 50m (165ft.).

Today, it is not unusual for a school-age discus thrower to achieve a 50m distance relying purely on natural talent and a simple but regular training program which concentrates on general development. Fortunately, all our beginner school-age discus throwers possess in varying degrees power, mobility, endurance, speed, strength and coordination. All these qualities and their interaction form the foundation for the technique required to throw a reasonable distance, i.e., around the 50m mark.

As a beginner, the discus thrower need pay no particular attention to any one of these qualities in his training. His own raw talent and his own blend of strengths and weaknesses will take the thrower to an acceptable level before his own peculiar weaknesses form a barrier to further development.

Why is it that so many reach the 50m mark and so few are able to improve beyond this point?

This seems to be the point at which the athlete and coach need to begin concentrating on the introduction of specific elements of conditioning for the young discus thrower, rather than concentrating on the general elements.

It is more than likely that up to this point the young discus thrower has not had his annual training program organized in such a way that the application of training loads is proportioned between the volume and intensity of activities in the preparation and competition periods, with each period having its own clearly defined objectives and goals.

Whether or not a single- or a double-periodized year is being applied is not important. What is important is that the planning needs to be done carefully and requires constant readjustments and modifications, taking into account the unpredictable, such as illness and injury, and the predictable, such as exams and important competitions.

It is also necessary to alter training programs at the last minute so as to allow for adequate recuperation or restoration from the cumulative effects of fatigue. It is imperative to try to avoid injury and overtraining because it must be remembered that the general physical condition of these young athletes is not as stable as that of elite athletes; the intensity of the workload needs to be monitored closely.

The young discus thrower has acquired a good base of general physical condition due to the cumulative training effect of years of participation in all sports but it is now advisable for activities to be selected which are very specific or simulate quite closely the chosen event. The most suitable age for specifics to be introduced is 14 to 16 years, depending upon puberty and maturity relative to the individual athlete.

PHYSICAL CAPACITIES

It is possible to assess several discus throwers and find each athlete to have a different blend of the following physical capacities:

- Technique/Skill Level
- Conditioning/Coordination Level
- Strength
- Power

Each discus thrower is unique. The training method used by one thrower will not have the same training effect on another. Although training programs will have many common factors, each must cater to the individual, taking into account the specific needs of the individual's strengths and weaknesses.

In a well-structured and thoughtfully considered training program, the complex development of these physical capacities is constantly being balanced and counterbalanced, so that no one physical capacity dominates. The optimal, combined use of these physical capacities results in a perfectly coordinated and powerful throwing action.

TECHNIQUE/SKILL

Technique, or the level of skill, is perhaps the most easily identifiable weakness in any athletic event, particularly the throws. Elite level throwers have continually modified their technique till they have a refined, efficient, controlled and balanced movement. As a result, the movement looks powerful, yet graceful and easy.

In an inexperienced young discus thrower control, balance and efficiency of movement seem to be the most difficult to achieve, regardless of the style performed. It has been an age-old view that beginners need only be taught a "rough" or approximate version of technique. However, today, due to the vast research into the central nervous system and neuromuscular motor learning, this has been found to be incorrect, and the acquisition of a high level of technique or skill is vital in the early stages of learning.

It is very possible to develop performances in young throwers by emphasizing conditioning and maximum strength work. However, in the final analysis, when it comes to elite level performances and the ability to transform the athlete's full physical potential into the competitive movement, faults in technique act as the limiting factor in future development.

Needless to say, limitations in the performance of technique and poorly performed movements increase the risk of injury and thereby shorten the expected competitive life span of an athlete.

The whole movement must be mastered before the specific details can be practiced. In achieving distances of 50m it is reasonable to assume that an acceptable command of the whole movement has been achieved. Technique work must be carried out year round but with special emphasis in the latter part of the general preparation period and the initial stage of the competitive phase. It is during this time that it will be necessary to correct any major technical faults.

This is achievable by a high volume of throwing sessions with standard and lighter weight discuses and implements, such as small shots, sling bags, etc. There are a multitude of drills that can be used to promote the desired effect.

I will suggest only a few drills relative to the points of technique that I consider of great importance.

Balance

It is my view that control and balance at the beginning of the turn sets the tone for the entire throwing movement. Without this initial control it is impossible to land in an effective power position in the center of the circle and complete the final delivery action efficiently.

The initial windup at the back of the circle is important because it sets the pre-torqued position that must be maintained throughout the throw. The hips and weight remain between the feet and from this point it is easy to unwind to find the balance point over the left foot. It is vital that the left arm and the left foot remain locked together in the same plane (for a right-handed thrower).

Moving too far over the right leg during the windup can make it difficult to achieve balance when the right foot is lifted off the ground. Balance at this point allows the right leg to drive through and create the power that will be released to the discus upon delivery.

Control

Concentrating on control over the left shoulder and the left leg helps to resolve some major problems. One problem is over-turning with the upper body and the failure to maintain the torqued position initially created by the windup, which then leads to the shoulders preceding the hip and leg drive to the center of the circle.

Another is a collapse of the left shoulder instead of keeping the shoulders level. As a result, the upper body bends at the waist and there is a "falling" into the center position with the legs hopelessly trailing behind. Ultimately the thrower's high point in the orbit is in the direction of the right side of the cage, rather than in the direction of the sector, and fouls result.

Drills

One excellent drill is to simulate the windup as if starting a throw with a barbell weighing up to 40kg on the shoulders (elite throwers can use a heavier weight; however, for the school age thrower who has had two years weightlifting experience, up to 40kg is sufficient). If the weight of the body is too far to the right, then the weight of the bar will pull the athlete over the right foot. The shoulders are to be kept level and parallel to the ground.

Care should be taken to avoid injury to the knees when this drill is being used, and careful positioning of the body is essential so as not to develop any other faults. This drill can be extended and the pivot continued until the right foot steps through to the middle. The extra weight will not only increase special strength relative to the discus throw, but also teach control of speed, which is a major area of difficulty for young discus throwers.

The main point here is to teach that slower and longer (i.e., the movement) is better than shorter and faster. The barbell across the shoulders is also an excellent point of reference when trying to keep the left shoulder and the left foot aligned.

It is also necessary to practice these drills without a barbell, as "dry runs" are invaluable for their applicability to specifics. They do not tire the athlete, and it is essential to do all technique work when the athlete feels fresh. Exhaustion only leads to loose, sloppy movements that are of no benefit. Pivot drills and the well-known "South African" movements are essential tools of learning and should be exploited to the maximum.

CONDITIONING

Historically, conditioning has been given a very low priority by many throwers, with strength and technique taking precedence in training programs. However, modern trends and current methods indicate that conditioning is now the most important factor. Throwers also are competing for longer periods of time than did their predecessors because of the higher levels of physical preparation.

Conditioning improves the efficiency of the body's response to the stresses imposed by progressively heavier workloads, and the whole body shares in these adaptations. The possibility of injury is reduced, and errors in technique do not arise due to compensation for deficiencies in the area of conditioning.

Conditioning is the foundation of all programs—whether beginner or elite. Modification of this foundation determines the heights of performance the thrower will achieve.

From the many aspects of conditioning, this text takes a look at mobility and strength.

Mobility

One basic element of conditioning is mobility. By definition, mobility is the capacity to perform joint actions through a wide range of movement. The result of mobility training is a greater range of movement in specific joint actions, or at least maintenance of the existing range.

A thrower with poor mobility will find it nearly impossible to learn to use effectively a new or modified technique. Inefficient patterns of movement and lower than potential performance imply poor mobility. Good mobility is of particular importance to throwing events, where the athlete needs to apply force to the implement over the longest possible range.

Therefore: Good Mobility → Freer movement → Efficient technique → Reduced energy demands.

Strength and Mobility

Strength training is particularly useful to the aims of specific mobility. Below is a selection of exercises suggested by Kim Bukantsev (Soviet Union):

• Lying or standing flys.

• Side bends with 5-15kg weight discs held above the head.

• Bench press with a wide grip (barbell) and dumbbell bench press.

• Dips with and without weight.

• Seated trunk twists with a 5-15kg weight held at 90° to the body.

• Jerks (either split or into squat position).

Discus throwing encompasses a great deal of rotational stress and the rotational and lateral plane of movement is easily overlooked. Most lifts in strength training are performed in a vertical plane, however, specific strength conditioning exercises allow for the rotational and lateral aspects of throwing to be developed. The importance of these exercises increases as the level of performance improves.

Strength

Strength is undoubtedly the one athletic quality which can be quickly and easily developed and can greatly improve performances in the beginner and intermediate level throwers. The introduction of strength training into the annual training plan of a 14- to 17-year-old thrower is paramount.

An important consideration, however, is that it must be within the capacity of the athlete, and therefore the coach must use each athlete's individual level of maturity and personal growth as a guide.

Since weight training must be considered in the overall development plan of the thrower, the training year should always be the basis of planning. The best method is to establish regular training cycles, each with clear aims and objectives; care needs to be taken to ensure that the young thrower will have sufficient recovery periods.

At this stage in a thrower's development, the two most important aims of strength work are the establishment of lifting technique and, perhaps more importantly, muscular balance. The establishment of a high level of absolute strength during the initial years of strength training is not important.

Absolute strength refers to the greatest possible strength a muscle can produce in relation to the dimension of its cross-section; this is independent of bodyweight. Experience has shown that, as a beginner develops a consistent weight lifting technique and training routine, strength levels will rise quite rapidly, using only light loads as the athletes body responds to the new training effect.

It is "relative strength" that athletes are concerned with—i.e., strength relative to bodyweight—and for throwers it is imperative that strength be increased without a substantial increase in bodyweight.

LOOKING AT THE DISCUS THROW

by Otto Grigalka, USSR

The author discusses some aspects of an orthodox discus technique and presents in detail the planning and organization of training with a comprehensive training diary.

A problem we have faced in recent years has been the inconsistency of our discus throwers in major competitions. Athletes often fail to reach even their training performances. Experience has shown that major competitions are won by athletes who execute a safe and powerful final phase of the throw.

It should be noted here that all discus throwers, men and women, produce excellent standing throws when in top form. Consequently, an athlete with a technically better standing throw has the advantage among throwers of equal standards.

Despite this, there are many athletes who believe in executing most throws in training with the turn. They are influenced by the training of hammer throwers and forget that the final delivery contributes over 80% to the discus distance (as compared to less than 15% in the hammer). There are also coaches who claim that standing throws have a negative influence on the total technique, overlooking the fact that an efficient delivery is usually achieved through hard work in winter with numerous standing throws into the net.

TECHNIQUE

One of the most consistent Soviet discus throwers is Dumtshev, who set a World Record in 1983 and has in his action several basic elements of a good technique. His technique, in several aspects similar to that of four-time Olympic champion Al Oerter, is presented in Figures 1 to 5.

Figure 1 shows how the athlete performs a very active entry into the turn with the whole "athlete-discus" system. This would not take place were the thrower to remain in an upright position and rotate around himself. Dumtshev avoids this "empty" rotation with an active body lean towards the throwing direction to create the necessary inertia that later influences his delivery.

The so-called passing phase follows the initial part of

FIGURE 1-5: DUMTSHEV'S ACTION

the turn. During this phase the athlete shifts the legs ahead of the upper body, which is moving toward the throwing direction. The aim of this movement is to create a dynamic position similar to that of a standing throw. It must be sufficiently active to prevent a forward drift of the throwing arm with the discus and a reduction in muscular tension.

As the passing phase is performed with the legs, there are three variations—stepping, running or jumping. Practical experience has shown that stepping is not acceptable in the age of fast throwing. A jumping action is responsible for a suspended turning in the air that is without ground support and therefore passive. This leaves running, a sprint with a turn within the 2.50 meter circle. Dumtshev executes it by placing the right hip "under the discus" and the right leg under the hip, performing a sprint virtually on the spot (see Figure 2).

The flight characteristic of the discus requires the implement to be directed as low and as strongly as possible forward. Consequently, all movements responsible for a flat flight are recommended and movements directing the discus high are to be avoided. This applies particularly to throwing into the wind, as is the case in the drawings, taken from a film of Dumtshev's action.

As can be seen in Figures 3 and 4, the hip and the right lower leg of Dumtshev are moving forward immediately after the left foot is placed on the ground. There are no lifting movements from the legs, no bending of the body and no lifting of the head. The athlete's lower body simply slides onto the left leg without a change in the relative position of the throwing arm to the shoulder axis. This creates pre-tension before the delivery. The drawings show this well.

Pre-tension can be achieved only when the athlete avoids a premature stretching of the right leg and the trunk, which usually occurs as a result of lifting the head. This needs attention, as the lifting of the chin and the head signals the stretching of all movement links. It is not wanted in the discus throw, particularly when throwing into a headwind.

TRAINING

Success in the discus throw, as in other events, is achieved through the cooperative work of the athlete, the coach and the sports medicine specialist, who are responsible for the following tasks:

1. Organization and facilities—the provision of suitable throwing areas and strength training facilities; the provision and quality of implements, footwear and clothing; the availability of filming and video equipment.

2. Training—the throwing volume using implements of different weights (standing and with the turn); specific power development exercises; general strength development exercises.

3. Coaching—the planning of training tasks; the establishment of technique fundamentals; the description of applied methods.

4. Medical-biological—self-control and medical control; recovery and restoration methods; prevention of injuries and illnesses.

5. Competitions—the establishment of a warmup program; the volume and quality of the warmup; the beginning and duration of competitions; be-

havior between competitive throws; weather conditions (wind direction and strength).

All these factors influence the final performance and should be recorded in detail in the athlete's training diary. The athlete is not to be left in a situation where the only information required, as some coaches believe, is made up of general training tasks, the number of repetitions to be performed in fundamental exercises and the total of tons to be lifted.

This often leads to situations where a certain training volume, responsible for success in one year, produces poor results in the next. Coaches often blame lack of psychological preparation for such shortcomings, which can be avoided by keeping a detailed training diary, as for example:

12/12/85   10am—warmup program No. 4. 10:20am—10 series of three throws with the turn (2kg discus, 5 to 6 minute recoveries), based on training task No. 8. After each series, technique drills No. 14 and No. 17. Best results: series 1—56.5m, series 2—59m, series 4 to 10—54 to 56m, etc.

The detailed entries must indicate exactly what has been done in a training day, as a vague outline is of little value.

Top performances in important competitions require confidence and therefore high-level training results. As training results are particularly important in the discus throw, adjustments have to be made to training to achieve this aim. However, it must be kept in mind that it is impossible to improve training performances and increase at the same time the number of training throws. On the contrary, there should be a carefully planned reduction of the training volume at certain stages.

For example, a thrower with a personal best of 60m is advised, in a training session, to perform 20 to 30 throws with an intensity of 57 to 60m, and not 100 throws in the 50 to 55m intensity range.

There is no need to condemn athletes who use high intensity and relatively low volume in training; nor is there any sense in asking an athlete to perform 15,000 to 16,000 throws in a season. Let's face it, even weight lifters have come to the conclusion that 40 repetitions of one lift should not be exceeded and have considerably increased their training intensity over the last 20 years.

DIARY DETAILS

The logical way to improve training performances is to set detailed training norms and methods in a diary format. All 365 days of a year must have detailed norms of what has to be accomplished. This applies to days of training, as well as days of rest, travel and competitions.

The daily plans are recorded in the diary by using a code that indicates by numbers the training methods to be employed. Explanatory information on other aspects, such as the implements (shot, discus, etc.) to be used, are added where required. Group 1, containing methods to improve training performances, can be made up of the following example:

1-1: Throws from the upcoming competition circle.
1-2: Throws from a training circle.
1-3: Throws from a bitumen area without a circle, net and marked sector.
1-4: Throws from the same area into a strong headwind blowing from the right side.
1-5: Throws from a wet circle or in the rain.
1-6: Standing throws with a 4kg shot into a net.

The list for Group 2 training tasks can follow this example:

2-1: Throwing of a 2kg discus.
2-2: Throwing of a 2.5kg discus.
2-3: Putting a 7.25kg shot.
2-4: Throwing of a 7.25 shot backwards over the head.
2-5: Throwing of a 7.25kg shot from the back of the neck forwards.
2-6: Throwing a 32kg weight with a handle.
2-7: Multiple jumps.
2-8: Vertical jumps.
2-9: Vertical jumps with weight.
2-10: Barbell squats.
2-11: Barbell half squats.
2-12: Accelerations.
2-13: Stretching.
2-14: Rotational weight exercises.
2-15: Barbell snatch.
2-16: Barbell bench press.

Additional information should include the time of day, the number and duration of the repetitions, training results and comments on technique.

Examples of Group 3 training tasks can include the following:

3-1: Tomorrow at 10am, intensive discus throws, 12 to 15 repetitions with 5-minute recoveries.
3-2: Tomorrow at 11:30am, 4kg shot throws into the net. Eight series of 5 throws with a full effort and 6-minute recoveries between the series.
3-3: Tomorrow's training takes place in front of rivals and spectators.
3-4: Tomorrow's training takes place in a paddock for recovery. The volume is 60 to 70 unmeasured throws.

3-5: Emphasis will be on the amplitude of preliminary swings.
3-6: Emphasis will be on the improvement of the hip action.
3-7: The task is to perform all throws without fouling.

The coach needs information on a variety of aspects related to training. Some of this information is collected on the field, near the circle or at the end of the sector where the discus lands, to provide on-the-spot feedback to the athlete. Other information comes from Group 4 diary entries and can include the following examples:

4-1: Hours of sleep during the night before a training session.
4-2: Time of breakfast and the number of calories consumed.
4-3: Medical problems prior to training.
4-4: Time of lunch and the number of calories consumed.
4-5: Medical help required in training.
4-6: Time of dinner and the number of calories consumed.
4-7: Methods used for restoration. Medical problems require additional information and should include diagnosis of the injury or illness and the treatment.

Group 5 covers information on competitions and can, for example, include the following:

5-1: Warmup procedures an hour or more before the competition.
5-2: Warmup procedures on the main arena.
5-3: Warmup procedures before the final throws and between the attempts.
5-4: The number of warmup throws and their quality.
5-5: The direction of the wind, the surface of the circle and the make of the discus used.
5-6: The detailed results of the competitive performance, including distances of every throw, final placement, names of main rivals and the evaluation by the coach.

It is important to record the exact conditions, as the wind direction and strength influence competition distances considerably. The difference between throwing into the wind and with a tailwind can be as much as 10 meters.

KINEMATIC CHARACTERISTICS OF THE DISCUS THROW

by Axel Knicker, Germany

The author stresses the importance of the movement structure in the analysis and training guidance of the discus throw technique and compares the techniques of the three medal winners at the Seoul Olympics.

The discus throw is one of the oldest athletic and Olympic events, though we can find very little scientific literature that deals with it. Only the delivery phase has attracted much attention, because it is responsible for the flight of the implement and therefore also the distance.

Unfortunately, the information about the release velocity, the release angle and height, etc. has only on rare occasion practical value for athletes and coaches in training. It provides hardly any guidance for concrete movement corrections. Such factors are only target values that can be influenced by the athletes. The performance control (training) aims to maximize the release velocity, while attempting to optimize the height of the release and the delivery angle.

It became obvious at the start of the performance diagnostics of the West German national squad in 1986 that an analysis of the target values was not satisfactory for individual athletes. Far more important was to discover the moments in the movement structure that are decisive in reaching the target values. The question was, "How must an athlete move himself and the discus in order to achieve the maximal throwing distance?"

The performance diagnostics between 1986 and 1990 were restricted, with only a few exceptions, to cinematographic analyses of competitions. This took place in order to collect data on selected athletes, as well as to make comparisons with international rivals. The analysis concentrated on the following main points:

- Time analysis of the duration of:

  a) Single support starting phase—phase 2.

  b) Unsupported phase (when existent)—phase 3.

  c) Single support delivery phase—phase 4.

  d) Double support delivery phase—phase 5.

(The double-support starting phase was eliminated because its influence is limited.)

- The vertical course of the center of gravity.

- The comparison of the target and the actual direction of the throw.

- The speed graph of the discus (vertical and horizontal parts).

- The angles of twist between the throwing-arm-shoulder and shoulder-hip.

COMPARISON OF THE TECHNIQUE OF THE SEOUL OLYMPIC MEDALISTS

Here an attempt is made to compare the three medal winners of the Seoul Olympics, based on the available data. These three throwers represent the top performers of the 1980's. In Seoul, Romas Ubartas collected the silver medal, Rolf Danneberg, the Los Angeles Olympic winner, finished with the bronze, only 10cm behind Ubartas, and Jürgen Schult is the World Record holder, Olympic champion and European champion.

The time characteristics (see Table 1) show clearly that all three throwers strove to make use of a short unsupported phase (phase 3). All the values are below 100ms. Schult and Ubartas use a single-support phase that is longer in duration than that of double-support prior to the delivery. By contrast, the double-support phase before the delivery of Danneberg is longer than his single-support phase. He also makes use of a considerably longer acceleration path in the double-support phase (s = 3.34m) than

TABLE 1: THE DURATION OF ACCELERATION (S) IN THE TIME CHARACTERISTICS OF THE DIFFERENT PHASES.

Name	Distance	Phase 2	Phase 3	Phase 4	Phase 5
Danneberg	63.54	0.32	0.09	0.13	0.20
	61.76	0.33	0.07	0.14	0.22
	62.96	0.32	0.08	0.14	0.22
	59.16	0.32	0.09	0.21	0.16
	65.80	0.33	0.09	0.16	0.20
	67.20	0.33	0.08	0.15	0.21
Schult	59.92	0.39	0.06	0.28	0.16
	67.40	0.40	0.06	0.28	0.13
Ubartas	66.12	0.32	0.09	0.21	0.16

TABLE 2: DISCUS VELOCITIES (M/S) AT THE BORDERS OF THE PHASES (FROM THE START OF SINGLE SUPPORT TO THE DELIVERY)

Name	Distance	Velocity	t1	t2	t3	t4	t5
Danneberg	63.54	Vm	5.7	12.8	9.8	9.8	23.9
		Vxy	5.4	12.4	9.7	9.0	20.1
		Vz	-1.7	2.3	1.1	-3.4	13.0
	61.76	Vm	5.0	12.1	10.4	9.3	24.5
		Vxy	4.8	12.0	10.2	9.1	21.0
		Vz	-1.4	1.9	1.7	-1.7	12.6
	59.16	Vm	6.8	10.7	11.1	9.4	24.0
		Vxy	6.0	10.4	11.0	9.2	18.8
		Vz	-1.6	2.4	1.7	-3.6	17.8
	65.80	Vm	6.0	12.5	16.3	11.7	24.9
		Vxy	4.2	12.5	16.1	10.8	19.1
		Vz	-1.1	0.8	1.9	-2.3	13.9
	67.20	Vm	5.1	9.9	11.4	8.0	25.2
		Vxy	4.8	9.7	11.2	9.7	19.8
		Vz	-1.6	2.8	2.2	-3.5	18.5
Schult	59.92	Vm	3.9	7.6	8.6	8.6	25.0
		Vxy	3.8	7.5	8.3	6.2	20.6
		Vz	-1.0	1.1	2.3	5.8	14.1
	67.40	Vm	4.23	10.2	11.2	13.1	24.1
		Vxy	4.2	7.6	9.8	10.3	20.0
		Vz	-0.6	1.9	2.6	-8.2	13.4
Ubartas	66.12	Vm	6.4	8.5	8.6	10.8	26.0
		Vxy	5.9	8.4	8.6	8.9	22.5
		Vz	-1.1	1.6	1.1	-6.0	13.1

Vm = Momentary velocity
Vxy = Horizontal velocity components
Vz = Vertical velocity components

Ubartas (s = 2.56m) and Schult (s = 2.53m). His discus velocity increases accordingly (V = + 177m/s), although, among the three athletes, Danneberg is the only one whose discus velocity decreases during the action. Both Schult and Ubartas increase their velocities from phase to phase (see Table 2).

The delivery action, traditionally emphasized in quali-

tative movement analysis, also shows individual differences in the performance of the best throws. In this area too, Danneberg differs considerably from Ubartas and Schult, who have the hip rotated forward already during the placement of the left foot. This results in a large angle between the shoulder and hip axis (Ubartas 50°, Schult 59°), compared with Danneberg's 23° (see Figure 1).

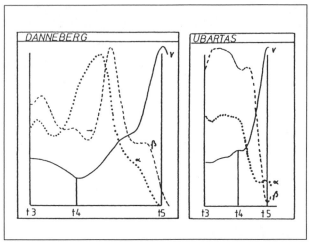

FIGURE 1: COMPARISON OF THE TWIST-ANGLE AND THE VELOCITY-TIME GRAPHS IN THE DELIVERY PHASE OF DANNEBERG AND UBARTAS

As can be seen, the angle between the shoulder and hip axis of Danneberg increases during the double-support phase in the delivery, while it begins to diminish after Ubartas has planted his left foot (t4). This naturally has an influence on the velocity curve of the discus. In case of Ubartas, the velocity curve shows a rise already in phase 4 (t3 to t4). Danneberg, on the other hand, suffers velocity losses until t4. His main acceleration takes place in the double-support phase in the delivery. Consequently, Danneberg's best throws are achieved when he can maintain the double support until just before the release.

The use of a double-support delivery by Ubartas and Schult can be regarded as positive because it apparently enables them to exploit completely the muscular pretension during the acceleration. The placement of the left foot into the throwing position is often responsible for the following single- or double-support delivery. A left foot placed in front of the right makes it anatomically impossible to maintain double support because the left foot is simply in the way.

This helps to explain the differences in the phase durations (see Table 1). Schult and Ubartas must cover a longer path with the left leg than Dannenberg in order to reach the delivery position. This lengthens the duration of the single-support phase.

A favorable hip and shoulder twist is the prerequisite for a fast final acceleration of the discus and a correspondingly short double support in the delivery phase. Danneberg, on the other hand, places his left foot very early, with the result being a short single-support phase. He must now keep his throwing arm and shoulder well back—an action that is reflected in a reduced discus veloc-ity—although the fast forward move over the hip helps to increase the angle between the shoulder and hip axis.

Nevertheless, even this "technique" leads to comparatively good throwing distances. This, in turn, reveals the problems tied to performance diagnosis that is based only on kinematics. In addition, the motor development of the athletes can be so far advanced that the variations in single characteristics appear in such a narrow range that it is difficult to evaluate their influence levels. Extreme differences can surely only be eliminated in training.

It appears possible and also sensible to formulate the demands of a scientific movement performance diagnosis and to establish kinematic analysis procedures as a means to guide training and competition in the discus throw. Kinematics has diverse possibilities in the guidance and control of training that can be used to optimize performance.

Grosser, Bruggermann and Zintl distinguish between five successive steps in the total process of performance control:

Step 1: Diagnosis of momentary performance and training stages.

Step 2: Establishment of targets and norms; planning of training and competitions.

Step 3: Execution of training and competitions.

Step 4: Training and competition control, self observations.

Step 5: Evaluation, norm comparisons, corrections.

In order to establish norms, it is first necessary to construct a profile of the demands of the event that identifies the performance-deciding characteristics of the event, as well as their relative influences on the target values. The estimation of the influence levels of the characteristics must be based on representative data from a wide range of individual performances in order to define reliable information for norms of individual techniques.

A regular kinematic analysis of, for example, the major competitions of a year, makes it possible to compare the existing stage of the technique with the planned norms. The technique characteristics that can be easily identified are then used in training. The key positions, such as the "delivery outlay, or the "throwing position," can be established with sufficient precision and compared with each other. The results can be made available to the athletes shortly after the training sessions by simply restricting the number of single phases being evaluated.

SOME ASPECTS OF THE DISCUS THROW

by Merv Kemp, Australia

Australian national coach Merv Kemp, who is coaching at the Australian Institute of Sport in Canberra, reports on some aspects of discus throw technique discussed at the European Athletics Coaches Congress in Aix les Bains, France, 1989.

Czech discus coach Jan Vrabel, speaking at the European Coaches Congress, was critical of the technique of many modern discus throwers and felt that they lacked the technical finesse of throwers of decades past.

In particular Vrabel was critical of the delivery action of modern throwers when compared to that of Oerter and Danek (coached by Vrabel). Modern throwers are inhibited by the size of the circle, and to avoid fouling they often have to check the forward/upward thrust and rotate away from the line of throw.

Possibly modern throwers:

- Pay too much attention to strength at the expense of technique.

- Because of their huge size, are lacking coordinative ability (c.f., the trend with hammer throwers and rotational shot putters).

- Undertake strength training which is too concentrated on general (squats, bench) rather than specific exercises with a technical basis.

But Vrabel also felt that the discus has inherent problems of a technical nature not experienced in the other throws:

- The final delivery action is more complex than the other throws, having rotational, vertical and linear components (c.f., shot—vertical and horizontal, hammer—rotational and vertical).

- Treachery of the discus technique. By this Vrabel meant the unreliable aspect of discus technique and that improvements in any particular aspect can be offset by other flaws.

BALANCE

Balance is important to good throwing. If the athlete is off balance, he can't vigorously launch into the delivery.

Poor balance at the point of release is exhibited by the athlete either:

- Falling away to the left.

- Falling out of the front of the circle.

- Falling back away from direction of the throw.

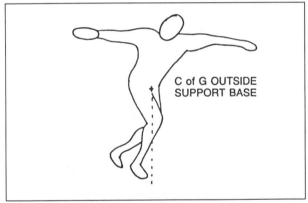

C of G OUTSIDE SUPPORT BASE

FIGURE 1: BALANCE

In the final delivery action a good deal of force must be applied to the right of the direction of the throw. The reaction to this will be to move the athlete left, off balance and possibly foul, unless this possibility is eliminated by the athlete being temporarily off balance in the power position. This, of course, does not sound correct, but remember that we are talking about a transitory position, one that the athlete passes through momentarily, coming back on balance at the point of the release.

POWER POSITION

How does one achieve the correct power position? It is the author's belief that the starting movements are very important and that the throw is set up at the back of the circle.

Preliminary Swings

The way in which these are carried out can be individualized, and a variety of styles can be seen in throwers such as Delis, Opitz and Savinkova. But basic principles apply that everyone should follow.

The swings should take the widest arc possible with the object of establishing torque between the hip and shoulder axes. With partial swings very little torque is established. Once created, the task, and indeed the main problem, is to maintain the torque throughout the whole throw.

During the windup, keep the hips between your feet and avoid getting too much weight on the right foot.

Entry into the Throw

At the end of the windup, hold the torqued position and move the bodyweight sideways from right to left. Think of moving the back of the left shoulder across and over the left foot to establish the balance point. At this point the right foot is just maintaining contact with the circle.

Great attention must be given to the movement of the left arm while moving to the left at the back of the circle. To avoid unwinding the torque and losing the displace-

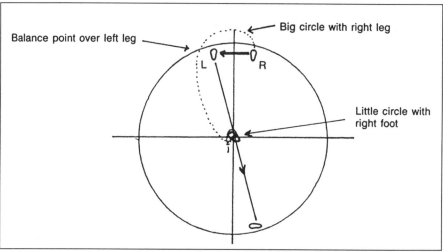

FIGURE 2: ENTRY INTO THROW

ment between the hip and shoulder axes, the left arm should lag behind the counter-clockwise turning left foot and left knee.

A common fault with many throwers is to commence the turning action into the center too soon, before the athlete has moved his bodyweight firstly over and onto the left foot. This is often accompanied and caused by an overactive left arm racing ahead of the left foot action, giving rise to an inefficient power position and a bowling action delivery.

The role of the left foot at the point of entry into the turn is particularly important. Mac Wilkins stresses that the pivoting action on the left foot should take place on the inner part of the ball of the left foot. A good rule to follow is "stay on the left foot as long as possible." The push off the left foot should come late.

At the back of the circle, the main action comes from the wide swinging and a very active right leg. Despite the success enjoyed by John Powell with his linear action, better results can be obtained by stressing the circular action of the right leg sweep around the left. This is the "big circle" path of the right leg, as described by Powell.

Wilkins advocates concentrating on sweeping the inside of the right thigh around the left leg and points out that many athletes lead the action with the top of the right thigh. When combined with an overactive left arm, the result is an athlete rushing into the center, landing off balance and unable to execute a powerful delivery.

The right leg should be actively swung towards the center and the right foot placed as quickly as possible in the center. The push off the left foot is delayed until the right foot is almost down again in the center. It is as if the thrower is to again establish a double-support position.

After pushing off with the left foot, the object is to very quickly ground it again in its final position at the front of the circle. Wilkins believes the left leg should remain bent and tucked in close to the buttock and then actively grounded soon after the right foot lands.

Pushing off the left leg too soon is a major mistake that causes the athlete to jump too much across the circle, to be

John Powell

74

too long in a nonsupport phase during which torque is lost.

A good power position is characterized by the athlete's torso leaning back over the right leg with the throwing arm held high so that the discus is at shoulder height. To achieve this position it is necessary for the right foot to lead the action across the circle and at the same time to keep the torso fairly upright. As the right foot is about to land, push the right hip out in the throwing direction.

Look for a shoulder-high position of the discus and a right angle between the throwing arm and the torso.

PATH OF THE DISCUS

Maximum release velocity requires that force be applied along the:

1. Maximum acceleration path

2. Direction in which the discus is moving.

For a good thrower, at the point when the left foot touches the ground the discus is at position A (270°). From point A, the discus moves down and back to position B before sweeping up to the release point at position C. With beginners the left leg takes longer to ground and by the time it does, the discus is already in position B, providing a clearly shorter acceleration path.

From position B to position C is an acceleration path common to both good and poor throwers. If an athlete improves his or her technique and shifts the discus from position B to A in the power position then, despite the technical improvement, distances may not be better because of other technical problems. The thrower is used to accelerating the discus only from position B to C and, as the discus moves down from A to B, the athlete may begin a linear movement forward with the left shoulder, shortening the radius and thus missing the opportunity of accelerating the discus from B to C.

Two choices are open to the athlete. Either learn to wait until the discus approaches B before applying force with the legs and upper body or learn to make use of the descending path from A to B by applying force along the path taken by the discus, that is down and against the direction of the throw. This is a short movement involving a lowering of the legs and upper body.

Try not to exert force in the direction of the throw too soon. Stress the rotational work of the legs, hips and upper body.

Summarizing

When the discus is moving down and back don't attempt to move the body forwards and upwards. The consequences of this could be:

1. Fouling as the athlete pushes himself through the front of the circle.

2. Incomplete right leg drive as the athlete strives to avoid fouling.

3. Turning away to the left with the left shoulder and spinning back into the circle in order not to foul.

Instead, stress the rotational nature of the throw and exert force along the path travelled by the discus.

DISCUS DRILLS

- Barbell on shoulders. Wind up as for throw. Pay attention to position of bodyweight and to keeping shoulders level, barbell parallel to the ground.

- Balance point. Barbell on shoulders. Step to middle with the left arm/barbell in line and trailing hips. Turn on inside of the left foot.

- South African drill stepping only to the middle with the right leg. Keep the head back over the left foot as long as possible. Bring the left foot to front and aim to get the discus up at least shoulder high in a power position. This can be achieved by tilting the body to the rear.

- Step from balance point to the middle and, keeping the bodyweight over the right foot, continuously pivot on the ball of the right foot, taking the left foot through to momentarily create a power position.

- Step from the balance point to the center again, keeping the bodyweight over the right foot; pivot on the ball of the right foot, bring the left foot through to the front of the circle and throw.

- Quarter turns, pivoting on the ball of the left foot, maintaining torque in each position after the initial windup.

- Block drill. Step up onto a 20cm high block with a bent left leg; stand up on the left leg and throw a 4kg ball.

SPECIFIC EXERCISES FOR DISCUS THROWERS

by V. Pensikov and E. Denissova, USSR

Specific exercises that are related to the actual throwing technique play an important role in the learning and development of technique and specific strength in the discus throw. In the following text, the authors outline the methodical background of specific exercises and list a number of suggested introductory and preparatory exercises.

Exercises aimed at developing a certain movement combination are known as specific preparation exercises. They are closely related to the structure of the basic movement coordination of the competition exercise, or they reflect one or several elements of it. It is important that specific exercises include elements that resemble the internal and external action of the competition performance.

Exercises that are based on an interactive development of specific strength and movement acquisition, and can be practically regulated, are therefore called specific preparation exercises. They enable considerable improvement of both the physical and the technical level of discus throwers.

Coaches can select from a variety of recommended exercises the most suitable and effective ones for the learning and development of discus throw technique and the acquisition of specific strength. Exercises that assist in improvement of the turning positions and the muscular tension during the key moments of the rotation are particularly effective.

Although the use of specific exercises is universal, their training effect is gradually reduced as an athlete's performance qualifications improve. Despite this fact, specific exercises are still beneficial for high-performance throwers in improving their technical elements, specific strength and specific coordination. All these factors are extremely important in the rotational movement structure of the discus throw.

Specific exercises also involve the throwing of different implements. In the winter, this throwing takes place indoors into a net. The weight of the implements should allow for a technically correct performance. The number of repetitions of an exercise is set according to the thrower's technical ability and preparation levels. The coach has to find the weak links in the athlete's technique and strength preparation to make the correct choice of exercises to eliminate shortcomings.

The nature of the introductory and preparation exercises becomes clearer when the importance of the basic phases and positions of the rotational discus throw technique in learning and training is understood. The exercises, as far as technique is concerned, must contain elements that are transferable to the movements of the competition performance.

Consequently, the chosen exercises should be based on the key positions of the throwing action to make the evaluation of their biomechanical effectiveness possible. These include the position at the start of the turn, the single-support phase, the unsupported phase, the final single-support phase and the position at the start of the delivery.

Every position in this rotational movement is characterized by the placement of the athlete's body segments in relation to the throwing implement and the tension created in the muscles. As the position changes, so does the tension in the stretched muscles.

An action as technically complicated as the discus throw is based on key movement positions that create the best possible conditions for a maximal performance. This occurs by joining all the key phases into the total throw. The total throw is successful if the athlete learns and develops a technique that eliminates, as far as possible, faults in the single elements of the movements and in the key positions.

In the establishment of classic technique, specific exercises are particularly important in the first few years of learning. It is only after the classic technique has been established that the athlete can afford to make changes based on individual demands. Also particularly important is to perform the exercises in a correct sequence of the single phases and in a certain temporal order of speed and rhythm.

The rhythmical structure of the complete throw is usually maintained by advanced throwers, although variations in the duration of the single phases take place. This is the reason for using different weight implements with different intensities to maintain as closely as possible the rhythm of the competition throw.

Further, the discus thrower adjusts his technique to the improved strength level, and this is responsible for changes in the technique. After all, the most efficient final performance depends largely on the strength level of the athlete's muscles, tendons and ligaments, developed by exercises in the key positions. This strength is known as the specific strength of a discus thrower, and the most effective means for developing specific strength are specific preparation exercises.

The learning and development of the starting single-support and the final single-support phases are the most difficult in the performance of specific exercises. The task of performing these phases correctly is demanding. The rotating and simultaneously forward moving system of the thrower-implement must create optimal conditions in the starting single-support phase for the body mass to move ahead of the implement and again should provide suitable conditions for the acceleration of the implement in the final single-support phase. The latter must occur with a fast placement of the left leg without a readjustment of the body mass. It is a task that requires specific coordination, strength, speed and muscular elasticity.

All these qualities can be developed through specific introductory and specific preparatory exercises. In employing these exercises, it is important to keep in mind that the duration of the above-described positions and phases will become contradictory as the strength level improves. As this can slow down progress, the total turning action should be executed in the proper rhythm at different speeds.

BASIC PREPARATION EXERCISES

Exercise 1—Sideways rotation into a half-squat position (lowest angle in the knee joint of 90° to 100°) with the feet placed wide apart. The weight of the barbell on the shoulders is 20 to 50kg. The exercise is performed at a slow speed. Attention is given to keeping the muscles involved in the hip extension continually under tension. The rotational action starts when the center of gravity of the body is in the center of the two legs. It reaches the maximum when the weight is shifted onto the support leg. The exercise is executed without stopping on the support leg.

Exercise 2—Similar to Exercise 1, but without a rotation. The athlete moves from one leg to the other, with the lowest knee joint angle in the 100° to 90° range, in a bounding action. The weight can be carried on the chest.

Exercise 3—Pushing of a light barbell from the chest up or forward while on the move. A push is performed every stride while standing on one leg. An intensive performance is required. The hips are not allowed to remain back and must be extended as the weight is pushed upward or forward. Attention is paid to the leg work, not to the arms holding the weight.

Exercise 4—Start sideways with the legs slightly bent and the feet nearly together. The movement takes place from the heels to the toes and from the toes to the heels. In this manner, a 10 to 15m distance is covered forward and backward in a straight line. The movement is executed by stressing the hip rotation without any shoulder action. The exercise can be performed without or with a weight on the shoulders (weight 5 to 10kg). The degree of knee flexion should remain unchanged throughout the exercise.

Exercise 5—Standing on one slightly bent leg, the athlete moves sideways by shifting from the heels to the toes and from the toes to the heels. All the details described for Exercise 4 apply.

Exercise 6—The exercise is performed while lying on one's back on a gymnastics mat with the arms extended sideways and the hands holding onto a support. The athlete rotates his or her legs and pelvis without moving the upper body. The legs should be kept together and no folding of the pelvis should take place.

Exercise 7—The athlete stands on the left leg with the outstretched right leg supported by a gymnastics horse and holding weights in each hand. The exercise is performed by jumping slightly forward onto an elevated (10 to 20cm high) surface without changing the left leg position. There should be no bending of the hips. The angle of the pelvis should remain unchanged.

Exercise 8—The starting position is the same as in Exercise 7, only the lead leg is placed on a lower elevation (40 to 60cm) and no jumping action takes place. The athlete simply performs a leg bend while holding a barbell on the shoulders and keeping the back straight. The support leg should be placed an optimal distance from the elevation to create tension in the hamstring muscles of the elevated leg.

Exercise 9—The athlete, standing with his feet shoulder width apart, executes forward arm swings (the action of the crawl stroke in swimming) with weights in each hand. The arm action is assisted by a half-rotation of the hips. The same exercise can also be performed in the opposite direction.

Exercise 10—Rotation of the hips and legs up to 180° (simple up to 90° and complicated from there to 180°) with a bar or javelin held in sideways outstretched arms on the shoulders. There should be virtually no changes in the angles of the hip and knee joints. The shoulder girdle should remain motionless and the exercise is performed fast.

Exercise 11—A rotational forward movement similar to the discus turn. The exercise is started with an optimally bent left leg in front. The right foot is turned 45° to 90° inwards. The athlete's sideways extended arms support a suitable load on the shoulders. The trunk is turned to correspond with the forward movement of the right leg,

which is placed the same distance ahead as it is in the discus turn. In the final position, the left shoulder is slightly lower than the right. The center of gravity is shifted over the left leg, and the right hip has to be at its highest point before the foot is planted.

Exercise 12—The exercise is started while standing on an elevated surface with legs shoulder width apart and knees slightly bent. The athlete carries a weight on the shoulders or hips and attempts to execute a jumping 180° turn. The legs and hips initiate the turn. The knee and hip joint angles should remain similar to those of the actual discus throw. The exercise can be performed with a reduced load by executing successive 90° to 180° jump rotations on one leg only.

Exercise 13—Running over hurdles using alternate lead leg action.

SPECIFIC PREPARATION EXERCISES

Exercise 1—Imitation of the final delivery action with an implement that is three to five times heavier than the competition discus. The exercise is performed in a standing position with only the final half of the delivery.

Exercise 2—Similar to Exercise 1, but with a full delivery action and an implement that is two to four times heavier than the discus.

Exercise 3—The exercise is performed in the final delivery position while holding a weight disc (5 to 15kg) with both hands. Avoid lifting the left shoulder higher than the right and stress rotation over an "elastic" left leg support.

Exercise 4—Standing on an optimally bent right leg with the left leg unsupported and the left side of the body facing the throwing direction, the throw is executed with the standard discus or other implements without allowing the left foot to drop to the ground.

Exercise 5—Similar to Exercise 4, but the throw is executed with a weight disc (5 to 10kg) held in both hands.

Exercise 6—Standing on an optimally bent left leg with the right leg unsupported and the shoulder turned slightly "inward," the throw is executed with the standard discus or lighter implements without allowing the right leg to drop to the ground.

Exercise 7—Similar to Exercise 6, but the throw is executed while holding a weight disc (5 to 10kg) in both hands.

Exercise 8—Standing throws with a limited rotation using a variety of implements (up to 10kg). Emphasis is placed on "catching" the implement with the right shoulder and keeping both feet on the ground.

Exercise 9—Standing throws with a preliminary backward cross-step with either standard weight or lighter imple-ments. The right leg is lifted at the moment the discus hand starts moving to the right.

Exercise 10—Throwing the discus or other implements with a discus turn that is started from a position facing the direction of the throw. Emphasis should be on keeping the discus back and on quickly placing the right foot after the drive from the left leg.

Exercise 11—Similar to Exercise 10, but the throw is executed holding a weight disc (5 to 10kg) in both hands.

Exercise 12—Similar to Exercise 10, but varied by taking a stride forward before the discus turn is executed.

Exercise 13—Imitation of a half-turn on a gymnastics form with or without light implements. The action is executed without stopping and while avoiding looking down.

Exercise 14—Separate or continuous rotations (90° - 180° - 270° - 360°) around the body's axis to the left (for a right-handed thrower), maintaining the basic starting position until the right foot is grounded. The initial hip and knee joint angles should remain unchanged.

SPECIFIC THROWING TRAINING

It is recommended that specific throwing training be divided into three categories according to their effect on the development of technique:

1. Throwing of implements with the highest effect (only standard discus).

2. Throwing of implements with a high effect (1.5 to 2.3kg for men; 0.75 to 1.25kg for women).

3. Throwing of implements with a limited effect (considerably heavier or lighter than the standard implement).

The use of flat surface implements is advisable in training because round implements (balls) change the sequences of muscular work, as well as the application of force and movement speed.

We recommend the following variations of combined specific throwing training sessions for reasonably technically advanced athletes.

Variation I (Preparation period)

1. Throwing of standard implements.

2. Throwing of lighter implements.

3. Local specific strength exercises.

4. Throwing of heavier implements.

5. Specific exercises using pulleys or rubber bands.

6. Throwing of the standard discus.

Variation II (Preparation period)

1. Throwing of lighter implements.

2. Local specific strength exercises.

3. Throwing of the standard implements.

4. Specific exercises with loads.

5. Throwing of heavier implements.

Variation III (Competition period)

1. Throwing of the standard discus.

2. Throwing of lighter implements.

3. Specific strength exercises.

4. General throwing of bars, weight discs, etc., or throwing of heavier implements from a standing position.

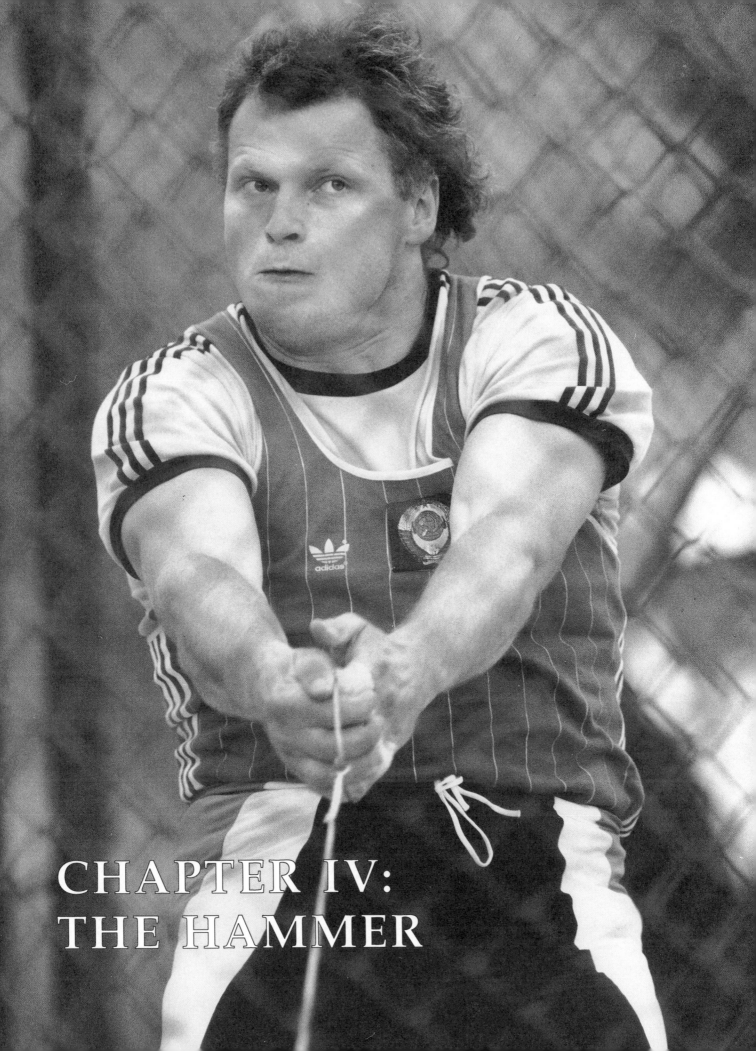

CHAPTER IV:
THE HAMMER

HINTS FOR BEGINNING HAMMER THROWERS

by Anatoliy Bondarchuk, USSR

One of the world's best-known hammer coaches discusses the learning and initial development procedures in the hammer throw, looking at different tasks and their correlations with the desired performance.

The format of the movements, as well as their content, make up the hammer throw technique. Coaches and athletes who underestimate this are making a grave mistake, because the learning of technique must occur parallel to the development of specific power. It should be added also that there is no correlation between the physical preparation level of an athlete and his form, reflecting basically different movement characteristics. Improved results in lifting weights do not guarantee better hammer performances.

Three methods—the whole, the part and the mixed approach— are used in the learning and the development of hammer throw technique. Most progressive and effective is the mixed method, where the learning of technique is based on a combination of the whole and the part methods. This is because it is rather difficult to execute the complicated movements of the hammer throw as a whole. The centrifugal force, even in mediocre throws, makes a rational distribution of power very complicated.

LEARNING PROCESSES

The learning process of the hammer throw takes place in three basic phases, namely:

1. The establishment of a correct image of technique.

2. The learning of the basic technique elements (preliminary swings, turns, delivery).

3. The development of the throwing technique.

Particular emphasis must be placed on the first learning phase, made up of the following tasks:

1. The establishment of a correct understanding of the basic elements of technique and the structure of the throwing rhythm. **Methods:** The explanation and demonstration of the technique as a whole and in parts (films, photos, drawings, videos).

2. The learning of preliminary swings. **Methods:** Swings with the left, the right and both arms (poles, hammers of different weights).

Suggestions: Attention in the preliminary swings is directed to the compensating movement of the body in the opposite direction from the hammer movement. When the hammer is situated on the right of the athlete, the thrower's body mass is shifted more onto the right leg. At the moment the hammer is in front or behind the athlete, the body leans a little back or forward, with the weight distributed evenly on both legs. The compensating shifts in the horizontal plane are important for an efficient transfer into the first turn.

It is advisable to perform preliminary swings at different speeds, observing that the lowest point of the hammer plane does not shift to the left. It must be kept in mind that this is not possible when the speed increases, forcing the athlete to let go of the hammer or break its movement by bringing it into contact with the ground.

The legs should be slightly bent and the arms stretched as much as possible, particularly when the hammer is at its highest point after passing the frontal plane of the shoul-

FIGURE 1 PRELIMINARY SWINGS

ders and the axis of the hips.

3.   The learning of the turns. **Methods:** Turns without the hammer and with hammers of different weights.

Suggestions: The hammer must be actively accelerated by the arms, shoulders and body in the double-support phases until the axis of the frontal plane meets the hip axis. This acceleration should continue even further in the transfer to the first turn. Every following turn should be faster than the previous one.

The movement of the shoulders and arms must be reduced as much as possible in the single-support phase, during which the athlete performs active work with his right leg and the right hip. This makes maintaining bal-

FIGURE 2: THE DOUBLE SUPPORT (ABOVE) AND THE SINGLE SUPPORT (RIGHT) PHASES IN THE FIRST, SECOND AND THIRD TURN

FIGURE 3: THE DELIVERY

ance possible and leaves the arms virtually straight.

4.   The learning of the delivery. **Methods:** Throwing of the hammer left-upward-backward after one, two, three or more turns. Throwing of weights with a handle and shots in the same way, using either both hands or just the left hand.

Suggestions: The author, personally, does not recommend teaching the delivery from one turn only, as the effectiveness of the delivery depends largely on a rational rhythm and the execution of the preceding turns. Athletes who can perform an excellent delivery from a standing

FIGURE 4: SOME SPECIFIC CONDITIONING EXERCISES FOR HAMMER THROWERS

position, or after one turn, will not succeed when they lack rhythm and have made mistakes in the turns.

In training, the learning and development of the final delivery should receive less attention than the preliminary swings and the turns.

5. The establishment of the whole technique. **Methods:** Throwing of hammers of different weights from three or four turns.

Suggestions: Attention in the teaching of the hammer throw as a whole is directed to the rhythm of the throw. Intensity is also important and learning should therefore take place with restricted or medium efforts.

Some maximum-effort throws at a certain stage of the learning process are acceptable, but should not exceed 10 to 20% of the total throws. It is also important to make sure that the hammer and the athlete are not turning together (as in the discus).

The development of hammer throw technique basically makes use of the same methods that are employed in the learning stages—namely the throwing of hammers of different weights. However, the number of low-intensity throws is reduced and employed mainly in the specific warmup. The number of medium- and high-intensity throws, on the other hand, is increased, with maximum-effort deliveries reaching 25 to 30% of the total. The main emphasis is always on a rational rhythm of the throws.

In general, it is advisable to begin training with low-intensity loads, followed by maximum and finally medium intensities. This is advisable because low intensities are effective in the learning of single technique elements, as well as in the development of the technique as a whole during specific warmups. Medium intensities, employed at the end of training, have a very positive influence on the recovery processes.

TECHNIQUE AND PHYSICAL CONDITIONING

The development of technique must occur parallel to the development of power capacities. An artificial separation of these two elements has a negative influence on the improvement of performances. It must also be kept in mind that good technique achieved through throwing with medium loads has little carry-over value to maximum-effort throws. Improved performances are therefore achieved by employing a gradually increasing number of maximum-effort throws.

Experience has shown that the world's best hammer throwers pay equal attention to the development of power and technique in all training phases of the year. Contemporary throwers do not divide workouts into strength, speed, technique, etc., training. This is one reason why the Soviet hammer exponents have, over the last 10 years, dominated the world rankings.

Coaches who advocate a separate development of physical capacities, are obviously ignorant of the use of varied weight hammers and of the fact that the employment of different intensities allows the improvement of physical capacities together with technique development.

Low intensities (20 to 50% of maximum) in strength development, as in weight exercises, have a positive effect mainly for beginners and low-level performers. As the athlete improves, so does his need for medium and maximum intensities. The number of repetitions in the first case (medium intensities) is around seven to 10, reduced, as the athlete improves, to three to five. Physiologists recommend not exceeding 20 repetitions in low-intensity lifts, as this will develop mainly strength endurance.

The principles used in weight exercises apply also to the throwing of varied weight implements—particularly to the heavy implements. It should be noted that the world's best hammer throwers systematically, throughout the year, used heavy (8 to 16kg) hammers to develop dynamic power.

The intensity of the throws with a normal weight hammer is based on percentages of the best training throw during a certain period of the year as follows:

low—50 to 80%,

medium—80 to 90%,

maximum—over 90%.

The best positive results are achieved by using during one training session two to eight maximum-intensity throws. The order of different intensity throws is made up of five to six low-intensity, followed by two to eight of maximum- and finally the required number of medium-effort deliveries.

TRAINING DERIVATIONS FROM BIOMECHANICAL STUDIES IN THE HAMMER THROW

by Manfred Losch, Germany

The use of implements of different weights and lengths is a universally accepted method in the development of specific strength in throwing events. In the following text the author presents the results of biomechanical studies conducted in the former German Democratic Republic on the problems and effectiveness of the employment of various implements in training hammer throwers.

OBJECTIVES AND PROBLEMS

The objective of the following article is to trace by means of biomechanical studies the direction of the training effect of specific hammer throw exercises (throws with hammers of different weights and lengths) for efficient training procedures. The author's own studies are here supported by the work conducted by Stacho and Schotte (1984).

The structure of the competition performance is regarded as the essential basic assumption in the development of fundamental as well as specific maximal and explosive strength capacities in the throwing events. This makes the movement execution and the movement structure (based on the general model of all four throwing events) the reference point for all observations.

Specific strength exercises must therefore be directed—beyond their role in developing energetic components—towards perfecting and optimizing the control and regulation of the neuromuscular system. This objective includes specific work aspects and contraction formats of the main participating muscle groups, as well as force applications that should correspond closely to the duration and level of the competition exercise.

Practical experience and scientific studies indicate that strength exercises designed to be finished with a braking effect have limited relevance for the performance. Furthermore, specific strength training demands, on one hand, the development of higher specific strength capacities through increased resistances. On the other hand, every effort should be made to minimize the interference of side effects that influence the dynamics of the competition movements.

From these imperatives follows the necessity of employing various exercises in training—above all throwing with hammers of different weights and lengths—in order to direct the adaptation processes as planned.

WORK HYPOTHESIS

The studies proceeded from the following work hypothesis:

1. The expected training effect from the use of longer, heavier hammers, which increase radial forces during the movements, is the development of specific strength capacities to maintain the balance of the thrower-hammer system.

2. The expected training effect from the use of shorter, heavier hammers—which increase tangential forces and, concomitantly, the share of kinetic energy transferred to the hammer head—is more efficient development of specific strength than is possible with the competition implement. This is because the shorter radius makes the angular velocity slightly slower than that achieved with the competition hammer.

3. From a combined employment of both implement categories we can expect:

    *   a high total mechanical performance and

    *   a limited interference from the side effects that

infringe upon the structure of the competition movements for an optimal development of event-specific strength capacities in unity with technical skills.

STUDY METHOD

An experimental and diagnostic analysis of the training of the leading hammer throwers of the former German Democratic Republic is used in this study, which employed a computer-assisted film analysis method. A projective rectification allowed the representation of single force components as analogous graphs.

The separate representation of F_{tan} and F_{rad} made it possible to ascertain tangential force components of hammers of different weights and lengths. Telemetric readings from the hammer grip provided additional information on the total forces acting on the grip. This procedure made it possible to reproduce separately the size and direction of the single force components.

The effectiveness of throws with 5kg, 6.25kg, 7.25kg (competition implement) and 8kg hammers (length 1.10 or 1.00m) and throws with short, 12.5kg (0.75m) and 15kg (0.60m) hammers was examined in comparison to their effect on the main parameters—total forces, tangential forces, travel time of the hammer head and angular velocity.

RESULTS AND DISCUSSION

Figure 1 shows the condensed median values of the tangential force per turn in the use of the various implements. It is noticeable that the tangential force, which reaches its local maximum in single turns and is the highest in the final turn, increases considerably from the 5kg

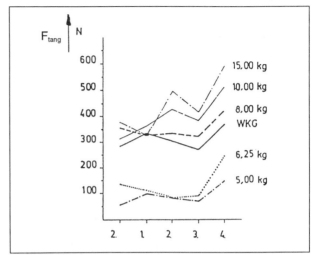

FIGURE 1: THE VALUES OF THE TANGENTIAL FORCE PER TURN IN THE USE OF DIFFERENT IMPLEMENTS (WKG = NORMAL WEIGHT)

TABLE 1: MAXIMAL TOTAL FORCE IN THROWS WITH DIFFERENT IMPLEMENTS.

Implement Weight (kg)		Length (M)	Total Force Max	% of Competition Implement(%)	Correlation Coefficient (r)	Significance (x)
Light	5.0	1.22	2280	84.4		
Light	6.25	1.22	2380	88.1	0.93	xx
Competition	7.25	1.22	2700	100		
Heavy	8.0	1.22	2810	104.1	0.89	xx
Heavy	10.0	1.00	2930	108.5	0.80	x
Short Heavy	15.0	0.60	2940	108.9	0.76	x

TABLE 2: THE TRAVEL TIME OF THE HAMMER IN THE LAST TURN IN THROWS WITH DIFFERENT IMPLEMENTS.

Implement Weight (kg)		Length (m)	Turning Time (S)	Correlation coefficient (r)	Significance (x)
Light	5.0	1.22	0.42		
Light	6.25	1.22	0.45	0.76	xx
Competition	7.25	1.22	0.46		
Heavy	8.0	1.22	0.48	0.74	x
Heavy	10.0	1.00	0.50	0.70	x
Short Heavy	12.5	0.75	0.50	0.70	x
Short Heavy	15.0	0.60	0.55	0.52	

hammer to the 15kg short hammer (from 150N with the 5kg hammer to 570N with the 15kg short hammer).

A comparison of the maximal total force in the throws with the various implements is shown in Table 1. As far as the total maximal force is concerned, deviations from the structure of the competition movement are particularly noticeable in the last turn with the short, heavy implement and the 10kg (1.00m) hammer.

The study results based on F_{tan} and F_{total} appear to indicate that the short, heavy implements should be given a special role in the development of event-specific strength capacities.

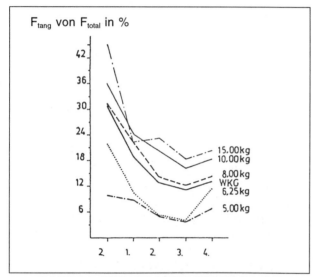

FIGURE 2: THE RELATIVE SHARE OF THE TANGENTIAL FORCE IN THE TOTAL FORCE IN THE USE OF DIFFERENT IMPLEMENTS (WKG = NORMAL WEIGHT)

Travel Time of the Hammer in the Last Turn

The studies show, additionally, that the total time taken up by the throwing processes and the corresponding time in the last turn are extended with the increase of the weight of the implement (see Table 2). The limited correlation coefficient of r = 0.52 for the short, heavy 15kg hammer indicates that the use of this implement does not allow for an effective rhythm-time structure in the performance.

It can be seen in Table 3 that short, heavy implements have registered higher average angular velocities than long, heavy hammers weighing over 9kg (the 12.5kg/0.75m implement has the highest value). Short, heavy hammers also have better acceleration performances than long, heavy hammers weighing more than 9kg. Furthermore, it can be seen that the maximal kinetic energy follows an increasing tendency up to the 8kg hammer before it begins to drop rapidly until the 15kg short implement is reached.

This clearly indicates that, as can be seen from the implements weighing more than 9kg used in this study, short, heavy hammers make it possible to perform closer to the competition exercise than the relatively long, heavy hammers in this same weight category. Particularly efficient in this respect is the 12.5kg (0.75m) short hammer.

Besides this, in regard to the tangential force and the total force, as well as parameters of the placement of the feet, a close harmony between the studied implements and the competition exercise can be detected. This essentially provides confirmation of the hypothesis formulated earlier in this text.

CONCLUSIONS

1. Throws with different implements that are heavier than the competition hammer are appropriate training exercises for the development of specific strength capacities because they essentially meet the demand of complying with the movement structure of the competition exercise.

The performance-deciding influence of these exercises comes from a complex effect on the development of specific capacities and technical proficiency. The observed effects of long, heavy implements (9 and 10kg hammers 1.00 and 1.10m in length) are:

- an improved specific throwing power through the development of the total and accelerating forces;

- a more stable thrower-hammer position in the turns;

- the realization of a dynamically long delivery.

TABLE 3: MINIMAL, MAXIMAL AND MEDIAN ANGULAR VELOCITIES, MAXIMAL ACCELERATION PERFORMANCES AND MAXIMAL ENERGY IN THROWS WITH DIFFERENT IMPLEMENTS (AVERAGE TRAINING VALUES OF THE ATHLETES BETWEEN 1986 AND 1988).

Implement (kg)	Length (m)	Angular min	Velocity max	(rad/s) x	Pa max (KW)	E_{kin} max W_s	Distance (m)
6.25	1.22	12.99	16.88	14.9	13.0	2712	82.58
7.25	1.22	12.96	16.67	14.8	14.9	2989	78.58
8.00	1.22	12.75	15.37	14.2	13.2	3046	71.24
9.00	1.10	8.19	14.34	11.3	8.2	2685	58.22
12.50	0.75	10.02	15.34	12.7	10.1	2462	35.86
15.00	0.60	8.67	15.04	11.8	9.2	2088	26.72

The undersired side effects occur from:

- a reduced acceleration performance;

- a diminished hammer radius as the result of the increased radial forces;

- a reduced angular path and delivery velocity (particularly large differences between the maximal and minimal angular velocities).

The observed effects of short, heavy implements are efficient in the development of specific throwing power (particularly the components of the forward drive) because the highest acceleration forces take place in the use of these implements. The mentioned undesired side effects appear in the long, heavy implements (over 9kg) in a reduced form, and the use of the 12.5kg short implement is more beneficial than the 15kg hammer.

2.   The throwing of different heavy implements does not lead automatically to the desired adaptive changes. The basic structure of the competition movement must be maintained and the employment of different heavy implements must always be tied to technique development tasks.

3.   Attempts should be made to use the variable method in different training units and sections in two or three categories in order to direct the training effect to particular structural elements. This helps to eliminate the danger of developing so called "heavy implement technique."

4.   Throws with implements of different lengths and weights have proven in the high performance range to be highly valuable when the variable method makes up 55 to 70% of the total volume of hamment throws. These exercises are executed in the greatest proportion in the maximal strength development phase as well as at the start of the specific training phase. The recommended periods for the use of long, heavy implements (9 to 10kg/1.00 to 1.10m) are:

- The general training stage: medium

- The maximal strength training stage: high

- The specific training stage: medium

- The performance development stage: limited.

The recommended periods for the use of short, heavy implements (12.5kg/0.75m, 15kg/0.60m) are:

- The general training stage: limited

- The maximal strength training stage: high

- The specific training stage: high (predominantly 12.5kg)

- The performance development stage: medium.

THE MAIN ELEMENTS OF MODERN HAMMER THROWING TECHNIQUE

by Eberhard Jaede, Germany

A detailed description of the principal technical components of modern hammer throwing, stressing an optimal lengthening of the double support phase as one of the most important contemporary technique factors.

From a technical point of view, performance of top level hammer throwers is decided by:

- rhythmically executed preliminary swings with the widest possible path of the hammer
- a smooth transfer into the first turn
- biomechanically soundly executed turns to develop an optimal rotational velocity
- a powerful delivery to reach maximal release velocity.

PRELIMINARY SWINGS

The hammer is pulled in a wide path from the left forward and upward. The lowest point of the hammer path follows an arc that begins opposite the toes of the right foot and finishes between the legs opposite to the throwing direction. The lowest point of the hammer is individually fixed, but the path must be lengthened in the transfer to the first turn. The path should cover the maximal distance with the left side of the body remaining fixed. This is particularly important when four turns are used.

It is known that the position of the lowest point of the hammer largely determines the angle of the plane of the hammer path. This, in turn, influences the length of the active acceleration of the implement and the widest possible path of it during the turns.

The speed of the arm circles is of great importance in the establishment of the rhythm in the preliminary swings, often performed below or above the optimal. If the swings are too slow, the thrower will never reach his maximal velocity in three turns. Preliminary swings that are too fast lead to the maximal turning speed in the second turn, after which the velocity drops in the third (last) turn. Both circumstances are negative for a good performance and upset an effective delivery. This also applies to throws using four turns.

TRANSFER TO FIRST TURN

The acceleration achieved from the preliminary swings must be effectively transferred to the acceleration of the thrower-hammer system. The athlete should during the transfer phase, therefore,

- further influence the implement in order to avoid velocity losses
- lead the implement on a wide path
- adjust himself for the changes in balance in the following throwing phases.

The active dissolution of the body twist begins when the hammer has passed the lowest point after the second turn and is tied up with:

- an active and correctly timed turning of the left leg
- a limited shift of the weight on to the left leg
- an emphasized lowering of the center of gravity.

As the hammer head passes the lowest point of its path, the right foot begins to turn with the turning axis being placed between the two legs. The pressure of the right leg and the whole right side of the body must continue in a circular movement to the left. The athlete must have a feeling that his body is rotating around an axis in the left side of it. During the transfer phase the upper body is bent slightly forward in order to shorten the hammer radius and to allow the upper body to remain close to the axis of the system.

At the end of this phase the right leg must perform a powerful but smooth movement in the direction of the rotation so that the weight is transferred completely on the left leg when right leg contact is lost. Attention is placed on the timely lifting of the right foot that should correspond to an approximately 50° turning angle of the hammer. An earlier action, in which the transfer occurs at the lowest point of the hammer, shortens the radius of the hammer path. A delayed leg movement in the transfer forces the upper body ahead of the hammer.

TURNS

The turns serve to accelerate the system thrower-hammer. A greater acceleration and high rotational velocity are achieved by top level throwers through three new technical elements that are achieved from improved physical capacities:

1. The lengthening of the double-support phase in order to allow the thrower to have a longer active influence on the hammer.

2. A conscious exploitation, in single support, of the turning hammer's inertia developed during double support.

3. The attempt to maintain the dynamic balance of the system thrower-hammer.

The lengthening of the double support phase in all turns is achieved in a relatively late lifting of the right foot from the surface when both feet are turned 50° to the left. The thrower also attempts to execute a fast and early placement of the right foot at the end of the single support phase. As this takes place, the shoulder and hip axis, as well as the connecting line of the toes, are no longer in the frontal plane. In other words, the right foot is not parallel with the left foot.

This is regarded as one of the important elements in modern hammer throwing technique, because it allows the athlete to lengthen the path of activating the hammer and shortens the single support phase. The active acceleration of the hammer in the double support phase follows from the moment the right foot lands until the transfer to the next single support phase. The shortening of the turning duration occurs, above all, from the shortening of the

Kevin Morris

THE TURNS SERVE TO ACCELERATE THE SYSTEM THROWER-HAMMER, ILLUSTRATED HERE BY TORE GUSTAFSSON, THROWING FOR WASHINGTON STATE IN 1986.

single support and the stabilization of the double-support phases. Admittedly, the radius of the hammer path should not be reduced during these procedures.

The time reduction of the single turns takes place gradually, about 15 to 20% at each turn. A forced or a limited change of velocity from turn to turn usually leads to a poor delivery phase.

The exploitation of the hammer's inertia in the single support phase requires the thrower to hang on to the hammer and to avoid any hip or leg actions. An active rotation on and around the left leg (support point) takes place as the hammer has passed the highest point of its path in order to reach the double-support phase as fast as possible.

A wide advance of the hip axis ahead of the shoulder axis, in comparison to the "old" technique, is to be avoided here. The whole body (except the arms) rushes ahead of the hammer with the heavily loaded left hip remaining fixed.

The ideal rotation of the whole system around a nearly vertical axis is the result of this changing relationship between the double- and single-support phases. A deformation of the hammer path and a twisted body position, common in the "earlier" technique, are avoided. It was responsible for a shortening of the radius of the hammer path, problems with balance stabilization, and consequently velocity losses.

The dynamic balance of the system thrower-hammer in the different turning phases is best achieved by keeping the hammer at a correct range, contact with the surface and active leg work. Active resistance to the continually changing pulling forces of the hammer is to be avoided.

The best throwers today turn with strongly bent knees to achieve the dynamic balance of the system, a wide hammer path and a better prepared position of the legs for the delivery. The trunk and knees position plays an important role in leading the hammer over a wide path. A close vertical trunk position is regarded as optimal. A backward lean shortens the radius; a forward bend needs muscular tension to hold the hammer and restricts acceleration.

The number of turns is decided by the technical ability level and the individual power devlopment of each thrower. Preliminary swings, responsible for the rhythm structure, deserve attention here. However, it should always be kept in mind that, whatever the structure, it must allow for the maximal possible acceleration of the hammer in the delivery phase.

If the maximal acceleration is not achieved with three turns, a turn can be added. However, if four turns fail to increase velocity, the speed of the preliminary turns has to be improved.

DELIVERY

The delivery is used for the final acceleration of the hammer and must be smoothly fitted into the total movement sequence. The modern delivery is divided into three phases:

Phase 1: The delivery phase begins with an active place-ment of the right foot. The center of gravity of the thrower is in its lowest position at this moment. The placement of the right foot must be executed actively in order to accelerate the implement effectively to its lowest point. The stretching of the leg should begin only immediately prior to the hammer reaching the lowest point to avoid giving away an otherwise valuable part of the acceleration.

Phase 2: The right leg continues turning left after the low point has been passed and pushes the right hip side in a striking movement forward—left against a rigid left side of the body. This allows the thrower to remain well ahead of the hammer.

Phase 3: The movement of the hip axis is suddenly broken only when it is getting close to facing the throwing direction to transfer the kinetic energy of the lower extremities to the trunk and the throwing arm.

CHANGES IN SINGLE TURNS

Some technical changes take place from one turn to the next due to the increased turning velocity and the increased centrifugal forces of the hammer.

- The centrifugal force of the hammer head grows proportionally with the increased track speed of the hammer. (80m throw—approximately 280kp). A higher centrifugal force requires a corresponding *centripetal* force, made up from:
  - Body weight
  - Muscular strength
  - Shifting of the trunk
  - Lowering of the body's center of gravity
  - Larger bend in the knee joints.

- The angle of the hammer path increases with each turn because of:
  - An increased shift of the trunk
  - Acceleration
  - the need to gradually adjust the angle to the delivery angle.

- The highest and the lowest point of the hammer shift from turn to turn more towards the direction of the turns (average value: 8 to 20°).

The hammer is thrown after three or four turns in the circle (2.135m) under an angle of 38 to 40° with the maximal possible delivery velocity.

STRUCTURAL TECHNIQUE ELEMENTS

The most important structural elements of an effective technique can be summed up as follows:

- *An optimally long acceleration path* can be achieved by striving for an optimal hammer radius through:

  a) A straightened arms position

b) Keeping the upper body close to the axis of the system
c) Counter movement of the hip axis against the hammer
d) An optimal rotational plane of the hammer path. (The angle of preliminary swings from 16 to 30° in the turns from approximately 20° to 38 to 40° in the final turn).

- A correctly timed lifting and an early placing of the right leg during the turns (under-turning).

- The lowest position of the thrower's center of gravity after the last turn has been completed (extended leg drive in the delivery phase).

- A release after a complete stretch of the body with surface contact.

A progressive acceleration is characterized by:

- A gradually increased velocity from turn to turn.

- Striving to reach an optimal throwing rhythm by an extension of the duration of the double-support phase (by about 10 to 20%) for an effective force application.

- An optimally increased velocity in each double-support phase.

- Minimal velocity losses in each single-support phase (not more than 8% of the achieved velocity).

- Reduction of the inertia influences.

- Elimination of undesired force influences by avoiding vertical fluctuations of the center of gravity and disturbances to the balance of the thrower-hammer system.

TRAINING THEORY IN THE HAMMER THROW

by William H. Freeman, USA, and Arne Nytro, Norway

A short summary of the training theory, main technical components and periodization in the hammer throw.

TRAINING THEORY

Throwing distance is affected by three factors:[1]

1. Release velocity

2. Release angle

3. Release height

The release velocity appears to be the most important factor. For a 246' thrower:

- a 5% speed increase will add 23' to the throw

- a 5% change in the release angle changes the distance by only 2'.

- The ideal release angle is 44°, though most elite throwers achieve an angle of 38°-40°.

It may be that a thrower cannot rise to the same release speed with a steeper release angle.

Maximum release velocity is achieved by lengthening the path that the hammer follows until it is released. The path is made longer by having a longer radius of rotation. This is done by:

1. The counter position of the pelvis

2. Extended arms and a relaxed shoulder girdle

   - By bending the knees, thereby dropping to a more "sitting" position during the turns, the radius of rotation is made longer.

   - By extending the arms to their maximum length, while relaxing the shoulder girdle, the arms will seem to "stretch" to more than their usual length.

The result is a longer radius, longer pull and faster velocity of the hammer. Wide winds (preliminary swings) help to set the stage for this movement.

The thrower must minimize the single-support time (when one foot is off the ground during rotation). The hammer is accelerated during the double-support, pulled strongly downward as the thrower "collapses" the knee while the hammer is high in the air. On each turn the trail leg (right leg for a right-handed thrower) is picked up and touches down earlier than in the previous turn (see Figure 1).

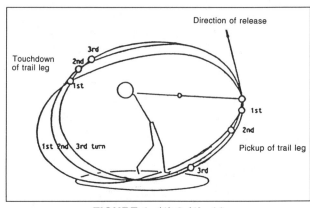

FIGURE 1 (1) 3 (1), 44
MOVEMENT PATH OF THE HAMMER

Efficient movement with today's technique shows these elements:[2]

1. The trail leg is swung closely around the pivot leg.

2. The distance between the feet decreases as the turns progress (from about 2' to about 1').

3. During all turns there is a relatively stable triangle between the arms and the shoulder axis.

4. The position of the shoulder axis relative to the hip axis is relatively stable.

5. The athlete's eyes are focused on the hammer head.

6. The stable rhythmic organization of the first to the last turn is characterized by the following:

   • The position of the hammer head during the trail foot's touchdown gradually shifts toward the high point.

   • As the turns progress, the low point of the hammer head moves toward the final release path (lower at the low point). The hammer throw is a very technically complex event. The East Germans tested prospects at age 13 (see Table 1). They believed that an athlete must train for 10-12 years to become an elite thrower.

Table 1: East German Standards for 13-Year-Old Hammer Prospects[1]

Height: 5-7

Weight: 121-137 lbs[3(1), 50]

Arm span: At least 2" more than height

30m (crouch start): 4.8 secs

30m (flying start): 4.0 secs

60m (crouch start): 8.8 secs

3 two-footed hops: 22-4

3 kg (6.6 lb) shot: 37-9

Note: Also test the flexibility of the shoulder girdle.

To make long throws as an adult, the technique must be engrained. To do this, lighter hammers are used, so the best junior throwers can reach 262-295' by age 17 (using a 3 kg hammer, compared to 16 lb for the regular hammer). The reason is that the mechanical factors for a 262' throw are the same, regardless of the weight of the implement. Thus, the athlete learns the technique of the throw by repeating it with an implement that is light enough to allow him to throw that far, if his technique is correct.

The East Germans note that "the experiences of the world's best hammer throwers show the great advantages of light implements as far as the perfection of the specific movement capacities and technique are concerned. The aim of the training of young hammer throwers is to achieve long throwing distances without a marked degree of strength development."[3] Table 2 shows their throwing goals for ages 13-17.

Table 2: East German Performance Goals for Young Throwers[(1)3(1) 50]

Age	Meet Hammer	Distance	Light Hammer	Distance
13	3 kg	55m (180')	2 kg	60 (197')
14	4 kg	60 (197')	3 kg	66 (217')
15	5 kg	62 (203)	3 kg	74 (243')
16	6.25 kg	62 (203')	3 kg	80 (252')
17	6.25 kg	68 (223')	3 kg	86-90 (282'-295')

Training uses technique units with drills using:

• wooden sticks

• leather balls with straps or wires

• medicine balls

• light (2 kg) hammers.

Each technical unit must be mastered before the next is attempted, with much use of part-whole learning. Sprint and jump training are used, along with event-specific conditioning and stretching exercises.

For adults, more use is made of strength and speed-strength training. Specific strength training falls into three categories:

1. Throwing hammers

   • different weights, 1-4 turns

2. Strength exercises for shoulder, trunk and legs (similar to event movements).

   • standing diagonal throws
   • jumps with extra loads
   • trunk exercises with extra loads in swings and turns

3. Forms of pulling and leg strength exercises with barbells

4. Major exercises are:

   • snatch
   • clean
   • pull
   • squats

Throwers use a double-periodized year. Anatoliy Bondarchuk, the most successful Soviet hammer coach, divides the development of hammer throwers into three stages:[4]

1. **Initial Preparation Level: Ages 12-14**

   - 3-4 sessions per week, 90-120 minutes each

   - All-around development exercises, sprinting, jumping

   - Use of light implements (3-5 kg)

   - Shot putting (4-6 kg.) from different positions

   - Weight training

   - Maximum training load for single session:

     2 tons of weight lifted

     15-20 hammer throws

     25 throws with the shot

     500 meters of sprinting

Most training in first (50-80%) and second (80-90%) zones of intensity

5% of training load in higher zones

2. **Special Fundamental Preparation Level: Ages 14-18**

   - 5-8 sessions per week, 120-150 minutes each

   - All-around development exercises, sprinting, jumping

   - Use of light (5-6 kg), normal, and heavy (8 kg) hammers

   - Shot putting (6-16 kg) from different positions

   - Weight training and special exercises

   - Maximum training load for single session:

     5-6 tons of weight lifted

Table 3: Weekly Cycle for Elite Hammer Throwers

Variant 1: 5 days, 10 sessions

Monday, Tuesday, Friday:

Morning Session:
10 mins warming up
12 throws with light (6 kg) hammer
15 throws with regular (7.25 kg) hammer
10 throws with heavier (9 kg) implement

Evening Session:
10 mins warming up
Weight exercises: 10 tons
Snatch: 1.5 tons
Twisting: 1 ton
Good morning: 1.5 tons
Half squat: 4 tons
Jumping from half squat: 2 tons

Wednesday and Saturday:

Morning Session:
10 mins warming up
30 throws with 16 kg weight (50cm handle), 1-2 turns
15 standing long jumps
50 throws with 16 kg weight in different kind
10 standing triple jumps

Evening Session:
10 mins warming up
Weight exercises: 5 tons
Twisting: 2 tons
Jumps trom half squat: 1 ton
Half squat: 2 tons

Thursday, Sunday: Rest

Variant II: 6 days, 12 sessions

Monday, Wednesday, Friday:

Morning Session:
10 mins warming up
10 throws with light (6.5 kg) hammer
10 throws with regular (7.25 kg) hammer
10 throws with heavier (8.5 kg) hammer

Evening Session:
10 mins warming up
Weight exercises: 8 tons
Twisting: 2 tons
Step test on bench with barbell: 3.5 tons
Cleans without splitting: 2.5 tons

Tuesday, Thursday, Saturday:

Morning Session:
10 mins warming up
100 throws with 16 kg implement in different kind
30 standing long jumps

Evening Session:
10 mins warming up
Weight exercises: 5 tons
Twisting: 1.5 tons
Good morning: 1.5 tons
Jumping from half squat: 2 tons
Playing games: 20 mins (basketball, volleyball)

Sunday: Rest

25 hammer throws

25 throws with the shot

1000 meters of sprinting

60-70% of weights in second zone of intensity (80-90%)

25% of weights in first zone of intensity (50-80%)

10-15% of training load in higher zone (90-100%)

3. Perfecting Acquired Skill Level:

- Ages 18 and over can reach 200 throws a day, but it has been found that 30-40 (sometimes 50-60) throws are sufficient.

The Soviet throwers mix light and heavy implements with the regulation-weight implement in all of their throwing events. Figure 2 shows a single-period macrocycle and the changing training emphasis of the different weights. Figure 3 shows a double-period pattern, again one that is appropriate for athletes competing indoors.

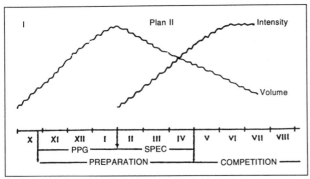

FIGURE 2 (11) 81 (1), 49
SINGLE-PERIODIZED YEAR FOR THE HAMMER

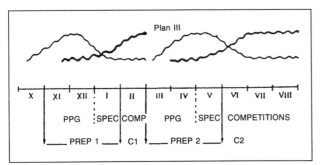

FIGURE 3 (11) 84 (1), 49
DOUBLE-PERIODIZED YEAR FOR THE HAMMER

Table 3 shows two variations of training by Bondarchuk for elite throwers.[5]

Table 4 gives another example of elite training loads, with the Soviet use of precise measurement of the training load. The athlete is Yuriy Syedikh, the World Record holder and Olympic gold medalist coached by Bondarchuk.[6]

Figure 4 shows the relative emphasis of types of training across the year, based on Soviet training theory.[7] Figure 5 shows a more general model based on East German training.

Table 4: Increase in Load Volume for Hammer Throwers

Year	1976 %	1980 %	1984 %	1984 Absolute values (9 months)
Training days	100	125	138	222
Total throws	100	118	151	6,332
Barbell training (tons)	100	170	198	1,402

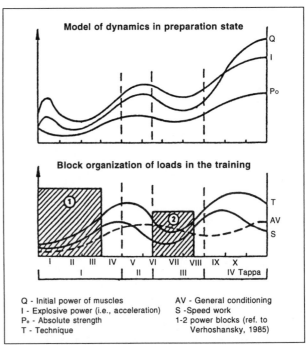

Q - Initial power of muscles
I - Explosive power (i.e., acceleration)
Po - Absolute strength
T - Technique
AV - General conditioning
S - Speed work
1-2 power blocks (ref. to Verhoshansky, 1985)

FIGURE 4 (5) 3 (1), 16
PERIODIZED TRAINING EMPHASES FOR THE HAMMER

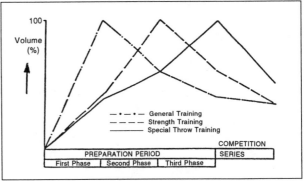

FIGURE 5 (1) 3 (1), 53
PERIODIZED TRAINING YEAR FOR THE HAMMER

The Eastern European sport bodies emphasize modeling in developing the training program for each event. This means developing a model of the specific skill patterns along with tests and standards that are needed to reach set levels of elite performance. Then the training program is designed to develop those traits, with the standard tests repeated regularly to measure the athlete's progress toward the standard. Table 5 shows the East German model for the hammer throw.[8]

Table 5: Model Items in the Preparation of Hammer Throwers

Throws		
16 kg weight (of 10 kg)	20m (24m)	65-7 (78-9)
18 kg hammer	48-50m	158-0-164-0
6 kg hammer	88-89m	289-0-292-0
5 kg hammer	93-95m	305-0-312-0
7.25 kg. shot, backward	21-22m	68-11-72-2
Jumps		
Standing long jump	3.40-3.50m	11-2-11-6
Standing triple jump	9.50-9.80m	31-2-32-2
Sargent jump	95-100cm	37"-39"
(jump and reach)		
Weights		
Squats	260-280 kg	573-617 lbs

TECHNICAL COMPONENTS OF THE THROW

The length of a throw depends upon:

1. The speed of the hammer at the moment of release

2. The angle of release

There are no aerodynamic factors, as in the javelin and discus. The speed of the hammer results from the thrower's muscular power, reaction time, coordination and physical stature. His ability to use this biophysical background to increase the hammer's speed from the winds through the turns until the release constitutes his technique. The angle of release also depends on the thrower's technique.

From a theoretical point of view, a tall man with a heavy build has an advantage in the hammer, but a small, powerful thrower can also succeed. The hammer thrower must develop optimal muscular power as a base for advanced technique, which takes years of daily training. Even then, he must continue to train to maintain his strengths and to try to overcome weaknesses.

PHYSICAL STRENGTH BACKGROUND

The hammer thrower must have overall strength, but these muscle groups should have special consideration in power training:

1. Legs

- the extensors of the hip (the gluteals and others)

- the extensors of the knee (the femoris group)

- the plantar flexors (gastrocnemius and soleus)

2. Lower body

- the twisters of the trunk (obliquus abdominis externis and internis)

- the muscles controlling the shoulders and arms (trapezius, rhomboids, deltoids, latissimus)

- the extensors of the trunk (erector spinae, quadratus lumborum

- the finger flexors

THE MECHANICAL BACKGROUND

If we look at technique as measured in terms of physical principles, the key word is speed, or velocity. The thrower tries to build up a high central speed, or angular velocity, during the turns by means of fast footwork. At the same time, he tries to maximize the hammer's peripheral, or linear velocity, by combining the central speed with a long radius. That requires long arms and a relaxed upper body. The body's axis of rotation is always moving forward in the circle and describing the outline of a cone (circumduction) (see Figure 6).

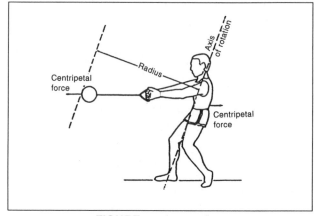

FIGURE 6 (12) p. 318
BODY'S AXIS OF ROTATION DURING THE HAMMER THROW

The fastest central speed and the longest arms give not only the highest speed of the hammer, but also the greatest pull outward (centrifugal force): up to 700 lbs for a throw of 200'. To control this force, the thrower must produce an equal (centripetal) force pulling in the opposite direction (see Figure 7). He must keep his knees bent and his lower back straight to control the centrifugal force exerted by the pull of the hammer.

To understand the relationship between the hammer's

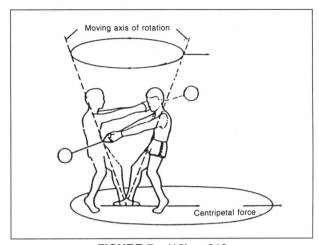

FIGURE 7 (12) p. 319
**BODY'S CENTRIPETAL FORCE RESISTS
THE HAMMER'S OUTWARD PULL**

speed and the angle of delivery, refer to the nomograph that Russian hammer thrower and engineer Anatoliy Samotsvetov constructed (see Figure 8). Such nomographs can help coaches discover their throwers' potential and correct their faults.

In Samotsvetov's case, he had measured a 200' throw. With a stopwatch, he had timed the flight of the hammer from the release to the landing as 2.9 seconds. From the nomograph he can determine that the angle of the release was 33° and the velocity was 82 feet/sec. But, using the nomograph, he can also see that if this thrower increased his angle of release to 43° with the same speed of release, he would have thrown 215 feet.

REFERENCES

1. K. Bartonietz, L. Hinz, D. Lorenz, & G. Lunau. (1988). The hammer: The view of the DVfL of the GDR on talent selection, technique and training of throwers from beginner to top level athlete. *New Studies in Athletics*, 3(1), 39-56.
2. Ibid., 47.
3. Ibid., 51.
4. William H. Freeman. (1989). *Peak When It Counts: Periodization for the American Coach.* Los Altos, CA: Tafnews.

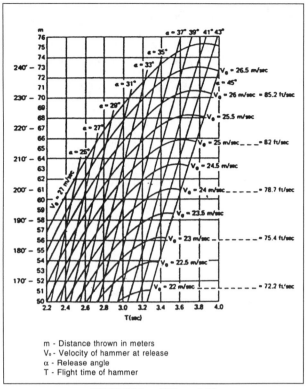

m - Distance thrown in meters
V_0 - Velocity of hammer at release
α - Release angle
T - Flight time of hammer

FIGURE 8 (12) p. 320
**RELATIONSHIP BETWEEN SPEED AND
ANGLE OF DELIVERY OF THE HAMMER**

5. Peter Tschiene. (1988). The throwing events: Recent trends in technique and training. *New Studies in Athletics*, 3(1), 14.
6. Bartonietz, et al., 55.
7. Tschiene, 16.
8. Ibid., 10.
9. Ladislav Pataki, Ed Burke, & Stewart Togher. (1989). The hammer throw. *The Athletic Congress's Track and Field Coaching Manual* (2nd ed., pp. 177-188). Champaign, IL: Leisure Press.
10. William J. Bowerman & William H. Freeman (1990). *The Track and Field Training Handbook.* Champaign, IL: Leisure Press.
11. Kevin McGill. (1984). Hammer Clinic. *Track & Field Quarterly Review*, 84: 1, 49.
12. William H. Freeman and Bill Bowerman (1, 74), *Coaching Track & Field*, Boston: Houghton Mifflin. By Permission.

A KINEMATIC ANALYSIS OF YURIY SYEDIKH'S WORLD RECORD HAMMER THROW

An analysis of the kinematic values of several technique parameters of Syedikh's world record throw at the 1986 European Championships in comparison to the corresponding parameters of a number of other world class throwers.

INTRODUCTION

Yuriy Syedikh (USSR) set a world hammer throw record of 86.74m in the European Championships in Stuttgart, Germany, in 1986. He had the following series: 83.94-85.28-85.46-86.74-86.68-86.62m! Two of his throws exceeded the previous world mark, set in June 1986 in Tallinn, Estonia. The high consistency of his series and the fact that no other thrower in the last few years has approached the distance, makes the evaluation of his best throw extremely interesting for coaches and sport scientists.

Selected throws of other athletes are used to evaluate the kinetic values of Syedikh's performance. These were drawn from 75 hammer throws of national and international athletes, recorded between 1985 and 1990 at the Cologne Sports Institute.

METHOD

The world record throw of Syedikh's and all other evaluated throws were captured by two high speed cameras with a frequency of 200 frames a second. This high frequency is required for an exact analysis, allowing for hundredth of a second accuracy. The marking of body segment points was based on the model of Hanavan. The center point of the hammer head and 22 body points were marked on each frame. The calculation of the three dimensional coordinates was made from the views of both cameras. The raw data was adjusted for the establishment of the path, angle and velocity characteristics.

The evaluations begin from the moment the hammer has reached its lowest point in the lead to the first turn and end with the final stage of the delivery release of the hammer handle. This establishes the scheme for the movement pattern of a hammer throw (right handed athletes),

as shown in Figure 1. The time points define the movements as follows:

    10 to 12 = Turn 1 (T1)
    12 to 14 = Turn 2 (T2)
    14 to 16 = Turn 3 (T3)
    16 to 18 = Turn 4 (T4)
    16 to 19 = Delivery Phase (R)

The single turns are divided into a double support phase (ds) (both feet in contact with the ground) and a single support phase (ss) (only the rotating foot is in contact with the ground).

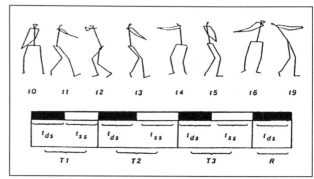

FIG.1: THE MOVEMENT PATTERN OF THE HAMMER THROW

T0—THE MINIMAL HEIGHT OF THE HAMMER HEAD BEFORE THE FIRST TURN
T1, T2, T5, T7—THE LAST GROUND CONTACT OF THE RIGHT FOOT
T2, T4, T6, T8—THE FIRST GROUND CONTACT OF THE RIGHT FOOT
T9—THE LAST CONTACT WITH THE HAMMER HANDLE OF THE LEFT HAND

DELIVERY PARAMETERS

The aim of the hammer thrower is to deliver the hammer at maximal velocity at an optimal angle. An optimal

102

delivery angle depends on the anthropometric measurements of the athlete and is close to 44° without velocity losses. How Syedikh solves this task is shown in Table 1.

Syedikh (URS) 86.74	
V_o (M/s)	30.7
V_oXY (m/s)	23.6
V_oZ (m/s)	19.7
α_o (°)	39.9
h_o (m)	1.66

TABLE 1: DELIVERY PARAMETERS OF SYEDIKH'S WORLD RECORD THROW OF 86.74M.

As can be seen, Syedikh's delivery angle (α) is 39.9°, about 4° short of the optimal angle. This means a theoretical distance loss of 0.5m.

The delivery height (h) of 1.66m appears to be low, but corresponds with the tendency to release the hammer at shoulder height. As Syedikh is about 1.80m tall the delivery value is in the range of his shoulder height.

We calculated his delivery velocity (V), as 30.7 m/s. The velocity of the hammer during all three turns, and in the delivery phase, is shown in Figure 2.

ROTATIONAL VELOCITY

A maximal velocity in all turns, particularly in the last turn, is required to achieve a high delivery speed. Information on this is provided in the time analysis of Syedikh's world record throw in comparison to other athletes in the same competition (Table 2).

The time analysis shows that Syedikh and Litvinov had the shortest total times of all competitors. They also achieved the lowest values in the last turn. All other evalu-

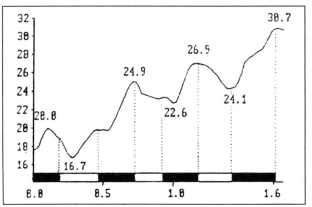

FIG. 2: THE VELOCITY GRAPH OF THE HAMMER (M/SEC) DURING SYEDIKH'S TURNS AND DELIVERY PHASES

ated athletes were significantly slower, as show in the examples of Haber and Schafer.

Syedikh and other technically advanced athletes attempted to keep their single support phases shorter than the double support phases. The presented example of Schafer, and the even more distinct action of Tamm (URS) (not shown), shows the opposite trend among technically poorer athletes.

This time distribution influences the length of the acceleration path, the distance covered by the hammer in the above defined section. It is shown in Table 3.

As can be seen, Syedikh has the longest time at his disposal to accelerate the hammer as 55.8% of the total time (from point t1) is spent in double support. This is particularly significant in the 6.68m long path of the delivery acceleration that is clearly longer than in other athletes.

The reason for Syedikh's favorable distribution between double and single support phases is in his extremely

	Syedikh (URS)	Litvinov (URS)	Schafer (FRG)	Haber (GDR)
T1 tds tss	0.44 0.20 0.24	0.44 0.15 0.29	0.45 0.17 0.28	0.47 0.22 0.25
T2 tds tss	0.47 0.26 0.21	0.60 0.35 0.25	0.60 0.32 0.28	0.51 0.28 0.23
T3 tds tss	0.43 0.22 0.21	0.44 0.21 0.23	0.51 0.21 0.30	0.50 0.25 0.25
T4 tds tss		0.43 0.22 0.21		
R	0.27	0.24	0.24	0.24
TOTAL	1.61	2.15	1.80	1.72

TABLE 2: A TIME ANALYSIS OF SYEDIKH IN COMPARISON TO OTHER ATHLETES IN THE EUROPEAN CHAMPIONSHIPS 1986 (SEC).

		Syedikh (URS) 86.74 m	Schafer (FRG) 79.36 m	Haber (GDR) 80.76 m
T1	tds	(3.61)	(2.80)	(2.75)
	tss	3.96	4.39	4.64
T2	tds	5.15	5.87	5.72
	tss	4.45	5.59	5.02
T3	tds	5.18	4.55	5.88
	tss	4.97	6.74	5.96
R	tds	6.68	5.91	6.07
TOTAL		34.10	35.85	36.04
RELATION tds toTOTAL (t1-9)		55.8%	49.4%	53.1%

TABLE 3: THE LENGTH OF THE ACCELERATION PATH OF THE HAMMER (M) OF SYEDIKH'S WITH COMPARISON VALUES.

		Syedikh (URS) 86.74 m	Schafer (FRG) 79.36 m	Haber (GDR) 80.70 m	Weis (FRG) 82.16 m
T1	HH Max	0.79	0.91	0.88	0.93
	HH Min	0.69	0.85	0.77	0.83
	Diff.	[0.10]	[0.06]	[0.11]	[0.10]
T2	HH Max	0.84	0.94	0.93	0.96
	HH Min	0.70	0.84	0.80	0.82
	Diff.	[0.14]	[0.10]	[0.13]	[0.14]
T3	HH Max	0.88	0.95	0.95	0.97
	HH Min	0.68	0.85	0.83	0.83
	Diff.	'0.20]	[0.10]	[0.12]	[0.14]
T4	HH Max				1.01
	HH Min				0.82
	Diff.				[0.19]
R	HH Max	0.92	1.03	0.97	1.05
MEDIAN		[0.15]	[0.09]	[0.12]	[0.14]

- HH Min = = > LOWEST HIP LEVEL
- HH Max = = > HIGHEST HIP LEVEL
- Diff. = = > DIFFERENCE (HHmax - HHmin)

TABLE 4: MAXIMAL AND MINIMAL HIP LEVELS OF SYEDIKH IN COMPARISON TO OTHER THROWERS.

early foot placement that is expressed in the azimuth angles (the hammer position in its 360° travel circle).

Syedikh reaches an average azimuth value of 63° at the liftoff and 224°(!) at the landing. His average acceleration path length is therefore 200° (=55%). This means an extremely long acceleration in the double support phase. No other hammer thrower has achieved such an early placement position, particularly immmediately prior to the delivery.

LOWERING OF THE BODY

Another important aspect in the technique of the hammer throw is the dropping of the hips at the moment the hammer reaches its highest point in the single support phase. Analogically the hips are lifted again when the hammer passes the lowest point in the double support phase.

Looking at the minimal and maximal height of the hips reveals that Syedikh has in 0.68m the lowest hip position of all athletes. This applies to the absolute value, as well as the comparison with other athletes of the same height, and is not correlated to Syedikh's physique.

Syedikh also has in 0.15m the largest average and in 0.20m the largest last turn relative lowering of the hips. Only Weis (FRG) and Litvinov among the world class throwers have values anywhere near Syedikh's. Tamm and Schafer have, in less than 0.10m, particularly poor values. These values apply to throws over 80m. Athletes in the 77m region and juniors show even greater faulty hip lifting action at the moment the hammer reaches its highest point.

	Syedikh (URS) 86.74 m	Schafer (FRG) 77.84 m	Sahner (FRG) 78.34 m	Weis (FRG) 82.16 m
T1	0.33	0.41	0.38	0.37
T2	0.30	0.36	0.33	0.33
T3	0.28	0.39	0.31	0.35
T4			0.31	0.37

TABLE 5: THE DEEPEST KNEE BENDS OF SYEDIKH IN COMPARISON TO THE OTHER THROWERS.

The prerequisite for an efficient lowering of the hips is a deep knee bend of the turning leg, a parameter that does not depend on the anthropometric factors of the thrower (see also Table 5).

Syedikh has here the best values in comparison to the other throwers, constantly improving his position from turn to turn. His extreme body position, combined with the lowering of the center of gravity, give Syedikh an excellent counterweight against the pulling force of the hammer.

ANGLE CHARACTERISTICS

The hammer throw technique is strongly influenced by the movement of the trunk and the position of the hammer in relation to the shoulder axis. A particularly important technical aspect is the size of the twist between the shoulder and hip axis (Figure 3) immediately before, or at the moment of the placement of the right foot. The lowest twisting values occur between zero azimuth and the lifting of the right leg.

The tendency to create a large twist in the single support phase, thus leading to velocity losses, and to then rebuild the twist in the double support phase to accelerate the hammer, is contradictory to Syedikh's action (see Table 6).

Syedikh reaches values of only about 30° in the difference of the maximal and minimal twist in the last two turns. In contrast, the two German throwers have differences between 40 to 60°.

A comparison of the 1987 and 1989 throws of Weis shows a clear reduction of the twist and there is virtually no trunk rotation in the last turn.

A comparison of the angle between the shoulder axis and the hammer wire at certain points is interesting. The angle is 90° at the point when the hammer is directly in front of the body (see Figure 4). It increases up to 150° during the "trailing" phase of the hammer. The comparison shows distinct differences in the techniques. Syedikh attempts to have a fixed position, allowing the hammer to move ahead or to trail very little (between 78 and 115°).

Schafer, with maximal values up to 150°, is an extreme example, although other throwers in our study, like Minev (Bulgaria), clearly showed the trailing of the hammer with values between 90 and 130°.

TECHNIQUE AND TRAINING CONSEQUENCES

The results of the kinematic analysis of Syedikh and the comparison values of other throwers show the follow-

All-Sport/Simon Bruty

Yuriy Syedikh

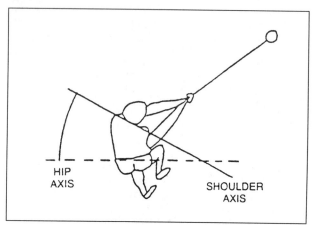

FIGURE 3: THE TWIST BETWEEN SHOULDER AND HIP AXIS.

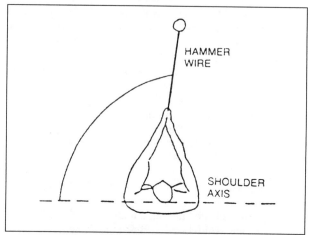

FIGURE 4: THE ANGLE BETWEEN THE HIP AXIS AND THE HAMMER WIRE

ing tendencies:

The release velocity, the release height and the release angle are mainly responsible for the distance of the throw. However, the delivery angle is negligible. Athletes, who are about 1.80 tall (Syedikh, Litvinov, Sahner) achieve their best distances from a maximal angle of 40°.

The highest possible release velocity is achieved through an optimally executed unwinding of the feet during the turn. The single support phase should be shorter here than the double support phase, particularly in the final turn. This is achieved by lifting the right foot when the azimuth is about 65° and an early placement of the foot when the azimuth is around 220 to 230°.

A maximal lowering of the body at the moment of the highest point of the hammer path is necessary to maintain high velocity during the turns. Besides, it is necessary to counteract the pull of the hammer with a low position of the knees, without giving up the vertical trunk position. A counter movement of the trunk would automatically lead to the shortening of the hammer radius.

Syedikh's technique shows that an optimal hammer velocity is achieved through a closely fixed position of the thrower and the hammer. A higher turning speed is clearly reached when the maximal twist of the trunk is between 30 to 40° and the hammer position remains a constant 90° between the shoulder axis and the hammer wire. The acceleration of the hammer takes place through creating and dismantling the distortion between the feet and the hip axis.

The development of the above mentioned technique criteria should begin early in the training of beginners. This applies in particular to the movement of the feet, the correct lowering of the body and the position of the hammer relative to the thrower. It should be developed correctly right from the beginning as relearning can later be extremely difficult.

		Syedikh (URS) 86.74 m	Schafer (FRG) 79.36 m	Weis (FRG) 76.30 m	Weis (FRG) 82.16 m
T1	Max	12	15	33	17
	Min	5	0	-2	13
	Diff.	[7]	[15]	[35]	[4]
T2	Max	45	64	62	55
	Min	15	17	3	13
	Diff.	[30]	[47]	[59]	[42]
T3	Max	39	66	55	43
	Min	10	18	14	14
	Diff.	[29]	[48]	[41]	[29]
T4	Max			49	35
	Min			8	22
	Diff.			[41]	[13]
R	Max	41	63	60	37
	Min	-13	-26	-9	-26
	Diff.	[54]	[89]	[69]	[63]

TABLE 6: THE SHOULDER AND HIP AXIS TWIST OF SYEDIKH IN COMPARISON TO OTHER THROWERS (°).

A BIOMECHANICAL ANALYSIS OF THROWS WITH HAMMERS OF DIFFERENT WEIGHTS AND LENGTHS

by Dr. Klaus Bartonietz, Germany

German throwing expert Bartonietz, presents a long-term biomechanical investigation of hammer throw technique, based on data from the world's leading exponents, and stresses the need to consider kinetic energy aspects in the use of implements of different weights and lengths implements.

In 1986, the World Record in the hammer throw reached 86.74m. In the near future, the implement can be expected to be thrown nearly 90 meters. The record performances of the former Soviet throwers have been accompanied by improvements in other international athletes, and female hammer exponents are preparing to enter the circle. All this has resulted in an ever increasing interest in the biomechanics of the hammer throw in training with hammers of various weights and lengths. This interest led to our study to determine the effectiveness of different training hammers.

METHODS AND PROCEDURES

Throws of Litvinov, Syedikh and other top athletes were filmed with two synchronized cameras in competition and training. An NAC motion analyzer was used to determine the space coordinates of the hammer head and the body of the thrower in order to calculate the time-related velocity, acceleration and angular velocity, as well as the radius of the hammer's path and several other parameters.

We estimated the error in the determination of the coordinates for the hammer head at +/- 5mm and assumed that with a stable frequency and equal phase of operation for the two cameras there will be a measuring error in the velocity values of +/- 0.05ms^{-1} and an error in the acceleration values of 0.5ms^{-1}. The estimate of the accuracy was corroborated by a comparison of the calculated force values for the hammer head with the directly measured values on a dynamometrical hammer handle. Training throws with hammer masses ranging from 5 to 17.5kg and lengths between 1.22 to 0.45m were investigated.

RESULTS AND DISCUSSION

It must be considered in the analysis of a hammer throwing movement that it is the athlete who exerts force at the end of the hammer on the grip. The action of the hammer head components on the total force summoned by the athlete are not identical with the forces acting on the hammer handle. According to the investigations carried out by Sataki and Slamka (1977), the acceleration forces acting on the hammer grip were 2.9 times larger than the acceleration forces affecting the hammer head.

From the physical relations between linear and angular velocities, and between radius and linear and angular acceleration of the hammer movement, it becomes obvious that the thrower must strive for an optimum relationship between the radius of the hammer path and the angular velocity of the hammer movement, so that, on the one hand, the peripheral velocity is as high as possible and, on the other hand, the athlete can keep his balance.

Figure 1 shows clearly the existing relationships between the peripheral velocity, the radius of the hammer path and the angular velocity of the hammer. Let us assume that the radius extension is limited, so the improvement of the release velocity—e.g., from 28 to 31ms^{-1}. for a throw of about 90m—is linked with a raising of the angular velocity by 2 rad s^{-1}.

	1st turn	2nd turn	3rd turn	4th turn
high points (degrees)	-8	-5	-12	-25
low points (degrees)	27	25	14	7

Angular differences— negative: shoulder axis in front of hip axis
positive: hip axis in front of shoulder axis

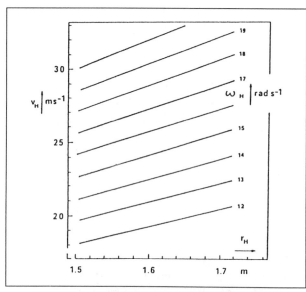

FIGURE 1: RELATION BETWEEN VELOCITY
OF THE HAMMER V_H, RADIUS r_H AND
ANGULAR VELOCITY W_H

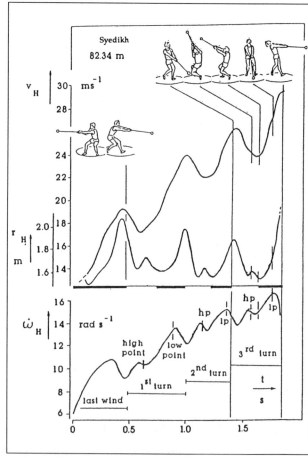

FIGURE 2: TIME-RELATED CHANGES OF
VELOCITY, RADIUS AND ANGULAR VELOCITY
OF THE HAMMER MOVEMENT

The real relationship between these parameters is exemplarily illustrated by Figure 2. The presentation begins with the transition to the first turn at the end of the last arm swing and ends in the release. The sections of double-support phases are set in bold type.

The figure shows that an increase in peripheral velocity during each separate turn is achieved by a radius extension. The angular velocity of the hammer and also of the thrower decrease at the end of the acceleration phases in the turns. From turn to turn, the increase of the hammer head's velocity and of the growing backward lean of the thrower's body are responsible for a decreasing radius.

The increases in force which must be generated by the thrower with each turn are shown in Figure 3. The momentary maximal acceleration and its centripetal components that compose the resulting force are achieved in the range of the low points of the hammer path. The leg muscle groups are therefore responsible for the impetus, while the trunk and the arms transfer the forces to the hammer head. The angular differences between the shoulder axis and the hip axis ("windups"), which must be relatively constantly maintained in the turns, are an expression of effective impetus work. Stronger "winds" reduce the radius of the hammer path and thus the path of acceleration.

Figure 4 and table 1 show the corresponding data. A relatively constant "windup" of 30° at the beginning of the second and third double-support phases can be seen in the throw of Syedikh.

Training must be directed to develop a perfect technique in interaction with the necessary development of strength capacities. Strength development includes the use of heavy implements for a large proportion of training throws. However, investigations of training throws with hammers of different weights and lengths has indicated that coaches and athletes must take into consideration the fact that the working conditions of the muscle groups

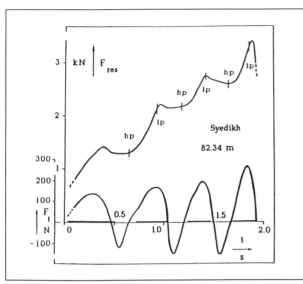

FIGURE 3: TIME-RELATED CHANGES OF THE RESULTING FORCE F_{res} AND THE TANGENTIAL COMPONENT F_1

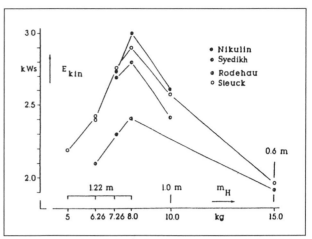

FIGURE 5: KINETIC ENERGY OF HAMMERS WITH DIFFERENT MASSES AND LENGTHS

TABLE 2: MAXIMUM RESULTING FORCES IN THROWING DIFFERENT HAMMERS OF DIFFERENT WEIGHTS AND LENGTHS (AVERAGE VALUES FOR 32 TOP THROWERS)

Mass	Length	Maximum resulting forces	
kg	m	kN	%
5.00	1.22	2.30	84
6.26	1.22	2.40	88
7.26	1.22	2.70	100
8.00	1.22	2.80	104
10.00	1.00	2.90	107
15.00	0.60	2.95	109

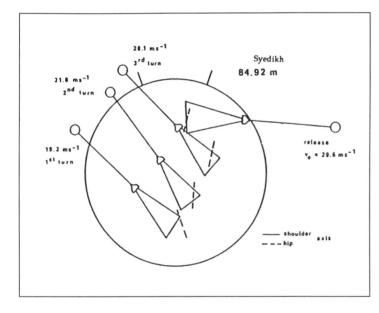

FIGURE 4: POSITION OF HAMMER, ARMS, SHOULDER AND HIP AXIS (PROJECTION IN THE HORIZONTAL PLANE) AND VELOCITY OF THE HAMMER AT THE BEGINNING OF THE DOUBLE-SUPPORT PHASES AND AT THE RELEASE

involved in driving are subject to changes when heavier and shorter hammers are employed.

The kinetic energy of the hammer, one of the most important biomechanical parameters, increases only when the hammer mass is below 8kg. Throws with heavy hammers in the 9 to 17.5kg range and with shortened wires lead to decreased kinetic energy. From the biomechanical viewpoint, the percentage reduction of the hammer length must be below the percentage increase of the hammer mass. This allows the heavy and short implements to have a positive effect in the development of specific strength capacities.

The data in Table 2 and Figure 5 indicate that hammers of lower than competition mass hammers are effective in the development of high-speed movement patterns.

These throws allow an athlete to realize a higher angular velocity and a longer path of acceleration. As a result of lower external resistance kinetic energy, power output and forces are at a low level.

SUMMARY

Our investigation during some years of training indicated that the specific movement patterns and the corresponding biomechanical parameter of the throws with hammers of various weights and lengths do not automatically change throws with the competition implement. The intended changes occur only when technique is constantly taken into consideration in the use of different implements.

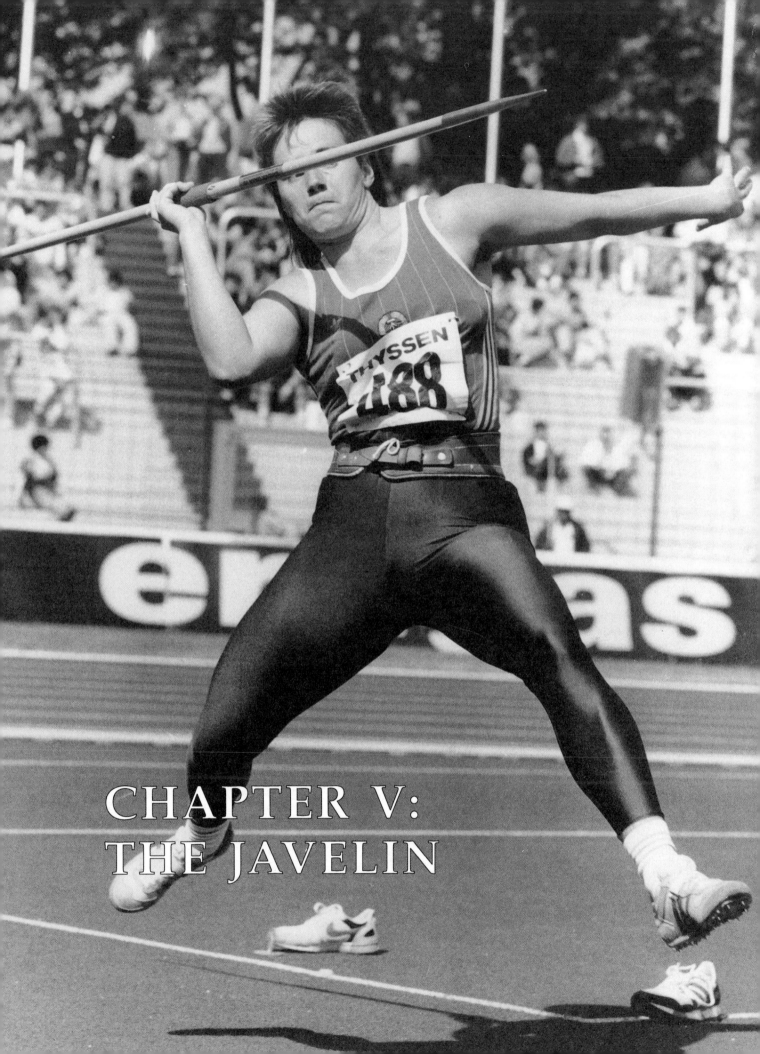

CHAPTER V:
THE JAVELIN

THE YOUNG JAVELIN THROWER

by Hans Torim, Estonia

Views on a multifaceted approach in the development of young javelin throwers with illustrated exercises and drills that lead to a natural basic technique.

The natural ability of throwing is developed in childhood by playing games. It is followed by a gradual process of learning to throw various implements before an individual javelin throw technique is established. This step-by-step development must take place with a corresponding improvement of physical capacities to secure an effective throwing action when the real implement is finally introduced.

A good thrower must first of all be a capable runner and jumper. Both of these abilities are essential for high-level performers. All throwing movements, particularly the delivery, involve the whole body. It is therefore important to develop strength and power in all muscle groups of the body, and not only in the muscles directly involved in the acceleration of a throwing implement. Clearly, multifaceted physical development is essential for future successes in the throwing events.

THE FIRST STEPS

Healthy children who have had the opportunity to be physically active are already by age 3 or 4 capable of performing such basic movement complexes as walking, running and even throwing. These basic movements are developed playing games, with those that involve simple activities with balls being particularly helpful in the later development of throwing ability.

As coordination of movements is at this age still very limited, with children finding it difficult to handle large or particularly small balls, it is therefore recommended that balls 10 to 20cm in diameter be used and that children be assisted in their attempts to throw and catch. They should first be taught to throw upwards with two hands and push a ball, or some other implement, from the chest.

A more advanced throwing action can usually be introduced around the age of 5 years, beginning with throws aiming at a target. The target is first placed on the ground and later at eye level for horizontal throws. The initial distance of approximately 1.5 to 2.0m is gradually increased. Different implements—balls, cones, stones, beanbags, etc.—weighing up to 200g can be used outdoors.

As children grow older it is important to increase the variety of ball games. Catching and throwing in pairs and in a circle lead to more complicated games that combine throwing and movement to encourage multifaceted physical development.

THE DECISIVE PHASE

The period from 7 to 13 years plays a decisive role in the development of throwing agility and capability as well as the development of basic physical capacities. The systems for guiding and analyzing movement make rapid progress during this period until children reach about 13 years, making it the best time for learning. It is the time when children are capable of learning the performance of complicated skills with ease, provided the skills are within their physical capacity limits.

Physical education studies have shown that the most suitable implements for the development of throwing capability during this age range are about the size of a tennis ball, weighing around 150 to 200g. Lighter (below 100g) and heavier (above 300g) implements had a negative influence on the quality of throwing movements. It also was discovered that target throwing produced biomechanically sounder movements than throwing for distance.

According to Danilov, the fastest development of a rational throwing action takes place from 9 years onwards. The stabilization of the throwing action occurs around the age of 11 to 12 years, leading to individual characteristics (signature) at the age of 13 to 14 years. While 9- to 10-year-old boys perform throws from a runup poorly, 11- to 12-

year-old boys are frequently capable of making good use of it.

Looking through the biographies of leading javelin throwers reveals that most of them were involved in throwing and throwing games while children. This allowed them already at the age of 14 to 15 years:

- to acquire relatively sound throwing skill

- to develop event-specific throwing speed

- to adjust the shoulder and elbow joint ligaments to the required tension and to maintain shoulder and trunk mobility.

According to the available information, the largest improvement of mobility occurs in the 7 to 11 years age range. Consequently it is helpful to frequently perform throws with a wide movement amplitude during this period.

It is significant that many high-level javelin throwers have at this age been involved in gymnastics and acrobatics that develop mobility and suppleness. Both of these factors also have been responsible for fewer injuries and stresses among javelin throwers later in their careers.

Injuries hardly ever occur in throwing games played by children, because they tend to stop the game or reduce its intensity automatically as soon as they become fatigued or bored. However, emotional participation in throwing games creates an excellent background for the development of throwing speed.

MULTIFACETED DEVELOPMENT

It is interesting to note that leading U.S. and Finnish javelin throwers have often participated as youngsters in baseball. Central European athletes, on the other hand, have played team handball. Other top-level javelin exponents, such as Olympic champion Janis Lusis, have benefited from volleyball, a game that has similarity to throwing in the spiking action and helps to develop leg power.

It must be stressed that most successful javelin throwers have at least up to the age of 15 to 16 years taken part in a variety of sporting activities. These activities have included throwing games (baseball, handball)—that, besides a variety of different types of throws, include sprinting and jumping for a multifaceted development—as well as other sports and a wide range of track & field events. Most have begun more serious javelin training at age 17 years, or even later, after they had established a wide and solid base for the event-specific technique and physical conditioning training.

All this indicates that early specialization is to be avoided in the javelin throw. It leads mostly to unnecessarily high throwing loads, single-faceted development and, sooner or later, to boredom. Even more dangerous are the almost certain chronic injuries to ligaments and tendons as the result of forced throwing loads and the lack of allround physical development that will later limit performance.

It is common knowledge that the winners of age-group competitions seldom excel when they reach adult age. A large number drop out, and those who continue produce only mediocre results.

Another important factor in the correct development of young javelin throwers is the choice of throwing implements. While boys at least can begin with a 600g women's javelin, the girls are frequently offered the same implement to start throwing. This approach is nonproductive and brings with it danger of injury. Even more foolish is to begin with throwing 50 to 60g tennis balls and then switch to 10-times heavier javelins.

The development of throwing can be effective and traumas are avoided only when the weight of the implements is increased step by step and adjusted according to the physical capacity and the level of the technique.

DEVELOPMENTAL EXERCISES

Learning the throwing technique should take place in a methodical order that leads from the simple to the more complicated performance. This takes place by using exercises and drills grouped according to learning and development tasks in the following five stages:

1. The establishment of a natural basic throwing skill.

2. The learning and development of the actions of gripping a throwing implement and pulling and extending the throwing arm.

3. Learning of the standing throw.

4. Learning of the throw from a runup.

5. Development of the total throw.

All exercises are described for a right-handed thrower, using the term simple implements for non-gliding objects, such as balls, stones, blocks, cones, light shots, sand bags, etc. Javelins, rods and long sticks are classified as gliding implements.

STAGE 1

The establishment of natural throwing skill is based on multifaceted (mostly playful and self-initiated) physical activities. This includes the development of a variety of movement skills, such as walking, running, jumping and throwing.

The development of throwing takes place in suitable throwing games and target throwing to help establish a natural overarm throwing movement and prepare the muscles and joints of the shoulder and arm for a more specific throwing load.

STAGE 2

The basic exercises for the learning and development of the pulling and extension action of the throwing arm include:

- Frontal throws of simple implements from a standing position, facing the direction of the throw. A bent and relaxed throwing arm performs the extension of the shoulder-arm-hand in a forward upward direction. Aiming for a target on a tree or a post is recommended (see Figure 1).

- As in the previous exercise but with the left foot in front. If balls are used, athletes should try to catch them on the rebound from the wall (see Figure 2 and 3).

- Target throws with a javelin. The target is placed 5 to 6m from the thrower, who aims the javelin directly at the target in the delivery position (see Figure 4).

- Extension movements of the throwing arm in a forward-upward direction without implements (see Figure 5).

- Extension movements of the throwing arm with a piece of hose or a stick against a tire or some other hanging object (see Figure 6).

- Extension movements of the throwing arm using an axe and a hanging object (see Figure 7).

- Frontal double-arm and sitting positions. The throws are first performed with a wrist movement, fol-

STAGE 3: EXERCISES 8-19

lowed by an arm and wrist movement and finally with the total shoulder-arm-wrist sequence.

Note: All the above exercises are performed without rotating the shoulder axis.

STAGE 3

The basic exercises in the learning of a standing throw include the following:

- Throwing of simple implements from a standing position with the throwing arm brought straight back and without turning the shoulder to the right. The delivery is combined with stretching of the legs and trunk (see Figure 8). The throws are performed:

  - Aiming for a horizontal target on the ground or a vertical target on a hillside, wall, tree or post.

  - Aiming for height over a volleyball net, pole vault bar or tree branch.

  - Aiming for maximal or preset distances.

STAGE 2: EXERCISES 1-7

- Throwing of simple and gliding implements from a standing position with the arm brought straight back and the shoulder turned to the right. The throwing arm, straightened in the elbow joint, is held above the shoulder axis (see Figure 9).

- Throwing of simple and gliding implements from a standing position with a correct withdrawal of the implement before the delivery. The throw is performed with a braking action of a slightly lifted left leg and a drive from the right leg and hip to form the "bow" position. The arm strike is fast with a high elbow (see Figure 10). The throws are performed:

    - Aiming for a parallel-to-the-ground flight path at targets on a hillside, throwing net, wall or post (see Figure 11).

    - Aiming for a gradually higher target to discover a suitable delivery angle (see Figure 12).

    - Aiming for maximal or preset distances.

Supplementary exercises recommended in Stage 3 are:

- Frontal double-arm medicine ball (1 to 3kg) throws with a leg drive, stressing the forward movement of the chest and shoulders (see Figure 13).

- Frontal double-arm medicine ball (1 to 3kg) throws from a kneeling position. The delivery occurs when the body is falling forward (see Figure 14).

- Double-arm standing throws of weights, small shots or medicine balls, stressing a gradually increased rotation of the shoulder axis and the trunk (see Figure 16 and 17).

- Standing throws of sticks, pieces of hose, etc. The rotation of the implement in the vertical plane indicates a correct delivery over the shoulder (see Figure 18).

- Single-arm frontal or rotating extension movements with an axe (see Figure 19).

- Exercises imitating the standing throw, stressing the "bow" position (see Figure 20-24).

STAGE 4

The basic exercises in the learning of the runup include the following:

- Throws from a 2- to 3-stride runup with the implement held back in the throwing position. An impulse stride is performed with a fast scissors movement of the legs, landing with the right foot turned about 45° towards the throwing direction (see Fig-

STAGE 4: EXERCISES 20-27

ure 25). This exercise is first performed from a walk, then from a slow run.

- Double-arm medicine ball throws performed in the same rhythm as the previous exercise (see Figure 26).

- Walking with a repeated withdrawal action of the implement. As the right leg moves forward, the shoulders rotate to the right and the throwing arm is brought straight back.

- Throws from four walking strides, including the withdrawal of the implement and the impulse stride. The athlete counts out loud: right-left (stressed)-and-throw (see Figure 27).

- Throws in a four-stride running rhythm, performed as in the previous exercise.

- Throws from a gradually lengthened runup by adding to and speeding up the pre-four-stride segment.

115

SUMMARY

In summary it can be recommended that the development of young javelin throwers should take place in four phases before specialization. These are:

1. The mastering of natural throwing ability—multi-faceted throwing and movement games.

2. Learning of the basic throwing technique with simple implements, using standing and running target throws and throws for distance—participation in throwing games parallel to the learning of the basic throwing technique and competitions in ball throwing.

3. Improvement of the throwing technique and adjustment to heavier and longer (javelin) implements—standing target throws and throws for distance (both standing and from a runup), as well as throwing competitions.

4. Further development of the javelin throwing technique and consideration of possible specialization—some javelin-specific training combined with all-round development (sprinting, jumping, hurdling) and competitions.

A JAVELIN STUDY

by V.I. Voronkin and E.V. Nazarenko, USSR

The authors analyze a study of the training methods used by Soviet women javelin throwers and come to the conclusion that an increased volume of full effort throws from longer runups should be responsible for improved competition performances.

Improvements in performance in contemporary javelin throwing are on one hand tied to an increased volume and intensity of the training load, and on the other hand to a better structure of training processes. Further raises of the performance level and possible successes in major competitions are largely dependent on the system of preparation employed by the athlete.

Studies and analyses of the training of women javelin throwers make it possible to discover how certain processes have been employed in the different stages of training.

In order to establish the distribution of the major training methods in the practical preparation process, we analyzed 23 yearly training cycles of women javelin exponents. The dynamics of the training load in the analyses were based on normal measuring units (km, tons, etc.), as well as on percentages from the total yearly volume (100%).

The training methods employed by the athletes were divided into five major groups, taking into consideration in the analyses of the throwing and running exercises the structure of competition performance (the javelin throw from a runup). The following groups were established:

Group 1

Exercises with the javelin and similar throwing implements

a) From a standing position, or from a 2- to 3-stride runup.
b) From a runup exceeding five strides.

Group 2

Exercises with assisting throwing implements.

a) From a standing position, or from a 2- to 3-stride runup.

b) From a runup exceeding five strides.

Group 3

Jumping exercises (single and multi jumps)

a) Depth jumps.
b) Standing jumps, as well as jumps from a 3-stride runup.

Group 4

Running exercises.

a) Specific javelin running exercises (with the javelin, over the full runup distance, etc.).
b) Accelerations to maximal speed (over distances up to 100m, accelerations, specific running drills).
c) Runs to improve speed endurance (distances exceeding 150m, cross country runs).

Group 5

Strength development exercises.

a) Using the barbell.
b) Using smaller weights.

RESULTS OF THE STUDY

An analysis of the information (see table) indicates that the yearly training of women javelin throwers places emphasis on the development of power and the improvement of the technical elements of the throw. It can be seen that the shares of the throws with the javelin and with assisting implements from a standing position or from a 2- to 3-stride runup (Groups 1 and 2) make up 54.1% and 25.6% respectively of the total yearly volume of throws.

% OF THE YEAR'S TOTAL VOLUME IN EACH MONTH														
TRAINING METHODS	Total 100%	Oct	Nov	Dec	Jan	Feb	Mar	Apr	May	Jun	Jul	Aug	Sep
Total throwing load	11363												
Standing javelin throws	2860												
	100	5.2	8.2	6.8	12.0	5.2	9.8	18.5	9.4	6.6	6.6	5.4	6.3
Javelin throws from a runup*	1728												
	100	5.0	—	—	19.0	4.0	5.0	5.3	13.4	14.5	13.7	12.1	8.0
Standing throws with assisting implements*	6202												
	100	1.9	18.2	23.2	14.3	8.0	13.5	7.4	3.0	2.6	3.3	1.5	3.1
Assisting implements throws from a runup* *	573												
	100	—	18.0	20.2	24.7	8.8	21.2	7.1	2.0	—	—	—	—
Jumping load—number of takeoffs	4694												
	100	4.2	8.3	14.1	13.6	9.4	6.2	6.0	12.3	7.5	7.3	5.1	6.0
Running load (km)	211												
Specific runs for javelin throwers	15.6												
	100	11.0	9.9	12.9	11.5	8.7	11.7	9.8	4.5	4.5	4.6	6.7	4.2
Maximal speed runs	48.3												
	100	4.3	11.7	13.6	13.2	7.3	10.1	6.9	5.3	9.0	7.2	7.1	4.3
Speed endurance runs	147												
	100	14.3	11.9	7.4	8.7	7.7	8.4	7.97	7.0	8	5	5.8	6.2
Strength loads (tonnes)	609												
Barbell exercises	381												
	100	8.4	8.0	9.6	14.0	7.3	16.8	9.6	8.5	5.3	5.0	5.7	1.8
Exercises with other weights	216												
	100	7.2	13.2	11.7	12.1	9.1	12.4	11.1	4.6	5.6	4.9	4.0	4.1
Imitation exercises (reps)	100	10.6	9.3	11.5	14.4	9.0	9.8	5.8	7.2	4.2	6.3	6.9	4.0

*including 2- to 3-stride runups.
* *runups over five strides

The volume of throws from a longer runup appears to be restricted because of the stress on the support and movement apparatus.

The development of endurance (69.7%) takes priority in running training, while specific javelin running exercises reach only 7.4% of the total volume of this group of exercises (Group 4). This proportion indicates that the athletes employ only a minimal number of exercises that assist in the development of the stride rhythm of the runup.

Exercises with the barbell (bench press, cleans, snatches and squats with maximal weights) make up 65% of the total volume of strength development training. Exercises making use of smaller weights are restricted to only 35% of the total volume. This distribution points to the leading role of specific strength training in the high-performance phase of javelin exponents. It can be assumed that such a distribution is most efficient for developing specific strength.

On the other hand, it should be taken into consideration that the predominance of strength development can have a negative influence on the development of other physical capacities. Consequently, the distribution of strength exercises should be adjusted to bring the development of the prime mover muscle groups to the foreground, without neglecting the leading physical capacities that correspond with the structure of the competition throw.

The analysis shows further that the volume of training in a year's cycle is based on characteristic changes in monthly intensities and loads. In double-periodization, the first phase in the preparation period lasts four months (October to January), and the second phase two months (March and April). As the first important competitions take place in February (the [former] Soviet Winter Championships), this phase is also the first competition stage.

The distribution of training methods in this structure is in the year's cycle characterized by a large volume of throws with assisting implements, then jumping and strength training prior to technical work (throws with the javelin and specific running training). The largest training load in the first preparation phase falls on running training in October. Throws with assisting implements, as well as jumping exercises and strength training have the largest share in December.

The contribution of running, jumping and strength exercises drops somewhat when technique development increases and the number of throws performed from a 5-stride or longer runup is virtually doubled. The development of technique therefore follows a large volume of work with assisting implements (work on single elements of the throwing technique), as well as jumping and strength exercises.

The training in the second phase of the preparation

period follows the principles employed in the first phase. Only the volume of barbell exercises (up to 16.8% of the year's total) and javelin throws from a standing position (18.5%) are increased.

CONCLUSIONS

The results of our study lead to the following conclusions about the structure of the training of women javelin throwers:

- The athletes at the elite performance level employ double-periodization in a year's training cycle.

- High-level performance is achieved by a large volume of training, employing several training methods.

- The athletes use in apposition heavy load volumes of specific power and technique development methods.

- An analysis of the planning of training showed that throws with the javelin (including similar implements) and assisting implements from a runup of more than five strides made up a relatively small share of the total volume in a training year—15% and 5% respectively. Here is, in our opinion, a hidden and unused reserve for a more effective training approach. A reduction of throws from the standing position and from a 2- to 3-stride runup and an increase in the volume of full effort throws from a longer runup appears to be the answer.

We believe that a successively increased volume of various training methods, combined with an increase of loads close to the actual competitive movement structure, would improve the efficiency of the training processes of women javelin throwers and with it their performances.

References include Russian language publications by:

Bondarchuk, A.P.
Verhoshanski, J.V.
Pimtrussenko, O.Z.
Matveyev, L.P.

JAVELIN TRAINING IN FINLAND

by Esa Utriainen, Finland

A comparison of the development and training of male and female javelin throwers in Finland, looking at physical differences, strength development, natural aptitude to throwing and periodization.

There are many structural differences between men and women and, in order to achieve good results, these differences have to be taken into consideration. Approximately 40% of men's body weight consists of muscle, compared to some 27% in women. Women are clearly shorter than men and proportionately women's legs are shorter. In general, women are about 10cm shorter, 10kg lighter and have legs some 25% shorter than men. Women's hips are lower, broader and also weaker.

Their bodies contain more fat and their strength level, proportionately measured, is 50 to 80% of men's strength. Because of their weaker support tissue, women run greater risk of injury. On the other hand, women are tougher and stand more pain than men.

The major differences, as far as the javelin throw is concerned, can be summed up as follows:

Weaknesses of Women Javelin Throwers (compared to men):

- A relatively small proportion of muscle mass to body weight and a larger percentage of fat.

- A significantly poorer production of testosterone, some 10 to 11 times smaller than men's.

- General weaknesses in the middle and upper trunk.

- Natural slowness because of smaller and weaker muscles.

- Generally poorer technical skills and implement control.

Strong Points:

- A greater capacity to train because of larger energy reserves.

- A better mental balance.

- Earlier maturity for intensive training.

Because of the above-mentioned differences, plus the menstruation cycle, a masculine training program can not be applied to women. The differences are so significant that special attention should be paid to female javelin throwers, particularly as far as strength, technique and speed capacities are concerned.

STRENGTH

In Finland, track & field talent is generally identified in the 14 to 15 years age range and then directed toward training programs at various levels. With practically no exceptions the girls selected for the javelin throw have a poor strength level. Strength is comparatively a minor problem as far as boys are concerned.

Generally, the first task of a javelin coach is to influence the athlete's attitude towards strength training. This applies in particular to girls, as it is much easier to make boys understand the need for strength and get them to begin weight training and gym work.

Strength training for girls during their first few years can actually be called muscle conditioning training. It must provide a careful and versatile start to strength development. Girls must be taught first to perform muscle conditioning exercises using only their own body weight for resistance.

To this is added medicine ball exercises and throwing of shots of various weights. Gradually, as strength levels begin to improve, girls are introduced to light weights and begin to learn the lifting techniques of various exercises. The most common exercises include the snatch, clean and jerk, clean, squat, half-squat and the hyperpull. A beginner normally needs one or two years to establish satisfactory control for performing the exercise listed above.

Artistic gymnastics, in addition to weight training, is one of the best strength development methods. It is particularly suitable for beginners but should be continued by experienced throwers throughout their career.

Boys, in general, are better prepared to take up strength training thanks to their superior condition. Furthermore, their attitude towards strength development is, as a rule, positive. Some might even see strength development as an end in itself, which certainly does not benefit actual throwing performance.

Because of the changes in the social structure from agricultural to urban industrialized society, the average strength level of javelin throwers has decreased significantly over the past 10 to 15 years. A survey of male javelin throwers, for example, indicated that seven out of the ten best Finnish throwers were able to clean 150kg in 1976. In 1986 only two of the ten best reached 150kg. No similar comparison is available for women athletes.

Compared to boys, girls at the same stage of training should perform more strength development exercises, if not in the volume, at least in the number of repetitions. The legs should not be forgotten, but emphasis must be placed on developing the upper body.

THROWING APTITUDE

Boys in Finland have a natural aptitude for throwing, as there is space for throwing virtually everywhere. In summer, boys throw pebbles into lakes or at cones in the woods. Winter is the time to throw snowballs. Due to this throwing experience from the childhood, boys find it easier to control the javelin and learn the technique faster and better than girls.

Both boys and girls play pesapallo, a Finnish national game similar to baseball. In this game, players throw a ball weighing 150 to 180g numerous times. As pesapallo is a very popular game in schools, it provides girls their main experience of throwing.

However, the throwing technique of the pesapallo ball can be considered to have a negative influence on javelin technique. The ball is light and often thrown below the shoulder level in a slinging action. This leaves the girls with little appropriate childhood throwing experience and they need a large number of throws to learn the javelin technique and control of the implement.

The actual technique is not as important in the beginning as the number of throws performed in order to develop throwing endurance and experience. Girls have only one way to improve their implement control—an increased quantity of throws. The importance of implement control can be seen by comparing the results achieved in throwing a 600g ball and a javelin of the same weight.

If the javelin result is better than the distance achieved with a weighted ball, the thrower has good control of the implement, which has different flight qualities. On the other hand, if the results with the weighted ball exceed the results of the javelin throw, there are certain technique and implement control problems, because the ball is easier to throw.

As boys, with only a few exceptions, achieve better results with the javelin, it is obvious that girls, who have had limited throwing experience, must in the beginning concentrate on throwing. At this stage quantity is more important than quality.

Presently in Finland 10,000 (±2000-3000) throws are considered to be an average for a training year. Of this total, 30 to 50% of the throws are performed with a javelin. The rest of the throwing, 70 to 50%, represents a variety of weight throws. Women normally use mainly underweight implements of 400 to 600g. Heavy implement (700 to 900g) throws are less frequent and make up about 10 to 15% of the total.

Men use a regular javelin and 800 to 1000g weights in training more frequently than do women. For the development of event-specific speed they employ underweight balls (400 to 700g), and, for the development of event-specific strength, overweight implements of 1 to 1.5kg, sometimes even up to 20kg.

Table 1 gives an annual distribution of throws with the normal javelin and underweight and overweight implements for both women and men at the age of 16 years and again at the age of 22 years. This is only an example and it should be stressed that variations occur depending on individual differences, as well as anatomical differences between men and women.

TABLE 1: DISTRIBUTION OF THROWS IN A YEAR.

Implement	Women		Men	
	16yrs	22yrs	16yrs	22yrs
Javelin	3000	5000	2000	5000
Underweight	3000	4000	1000	2000
Overweight	800	1500	3000	4000
Total	6800	10500	6000	11000

Finally, a few words about throwing exercises in training. We avoid standing throws after the first year of training, when standing throws are used only as a warmup for the work to follow. The main emphasis in the throwing exercises during the winter, when training takes place indoors, is placed on throws from a cross-stride approach and a 6- to 8-stride bounding runup (5-stride rhythm).

Some throws from a full runup are included in practically every training session. The number of these throws is increased as the competition season approaches.

PERIODIZATION

For many years, javelin throwers in Finland used a single-periodized year, divided into two basic training cycles, a pre-season cycle and a competition cycle followed by a brief transition cycle. This has now been changed to double periodization, where the first period finishes at the end of March with the national indoor championships and the second is terminated at the end of the normal summer season.

The double-periodized year is based on the following distribution of training:

Basic Training I—8 weeks with emphasis on general endurance, general strength and specific strength development.

Basic Training II—8 weeks with emphasis on maximal strength development and a large volume of throwing.

Pre-Season I—5 weeks with emphasis on speed (sprints), general and specific strength and technique development.

Competitions I—3 weeks with emphasis on explosive strength and event-specific speed development.

Basic Training III—4 weeks with emphasis on the same qualities emphasized in Basic Training I.

Basic Training IV—4 weeks with emphasis on the same qualities emphasized in Basic Training II.

Pre-Season II—6 weeks with emphasis on the same qualities emphasized in Preseason I.

Main Competition Season—July, August, September.S **Transition**—3 to 4 weeks.

122

SOME OBSERVATIONS ABOUT JAVELIN TRAINING

by N. Karatajev, Russia

Originally titled "There Are No Throws Without Throwing," the following text looks at the methods and means employed in the training of junior javelin throwers at the Volgograd Sports School.

Is it incidental that good javelin throwers often come from country towns? Of course not. Most specialists will agree that the best areas for the development of javelin throwers are close to rivers, lakes and mountains, where the natural setting allows children to throw stones virtually every day. They develop a natural basic throwing action at play, not in a forced learning situation.

It is possible in country areas to select javelin talent according to the distances achieved in stone throwing. Realistically, however, it is necessary to take into consideration the physiques of the children, their ability to throw stones or balls (weighing 100 to 200g), their flexibility and mobility, their sprinting ability (over 30 to 60m), and their capacity to exceed the jumping power of their contemporaries.

One of the problems, once the selection has taken place, is to eliminate previous faults acquired by novices during their basic training. These are often the result of poor coordination among coaches and the absence of a technical system. Vladimir Ovchinnikov is a typical example of what can be achieved when coaches agree on the basic methods of training and technique. When he joined our group, he improved 8.50m in eight months and 18 months later threw 80.26m, a new World Junior Record.

Unfortunately, there are far more examples of the first coach having failed to lead the young thrower to high-level performances. This author believes there is nothing new in the statement that novice athletes in all throwing events must be taught the same basic technique. This can then be followed by an individual approach in the development of technique, taking into consideration the physical characteristics of an athlete and the potential to improve these capacities.

TRAINING TASKS

Now to my own work with javelin throwers that has for several years been based on twice-a-day training where the daily tasks are repeated week in and week out. However, although the tasks are practically repeated, the training means vary continually, even if it might not be obvious at first glance. What follows is an example:

Monday: Improvement of the throwing rhythm, development of specific and speed capacities. Training means:

- Putting of shots, stones and different weights with both hands from a variety of positions.

- Starts, accelerations, runs with the javelin.

- Imitation exercises.

Tuesday: Improvement of the shoulder and arm action in the javelin delivery, development of agility, flexibility and mobility, development of jumping capacity. Training means:

- Imitation throwing exercises using pulleys and the javelin.

- Ball games, tumbling, gymnastics, hurdles exercises.

- Depth jumps.

Wednesday: Improvement of the javelin technique

elements (standing and from a runup), development of specific power and strength capacities. Training means:

- Throwing of the javelin, stones and shots (standing and from a runup).

- Imitation exercises with and without implements (standing, walking and running).

- Single- and double-arm throws of various weights from different positions.

- Complex weight training exercises.

- Different jumping and bounding exercises.

- Sprints (30 to 200m).

Thursday: Theoretical preparations, restoration. Restoration means:

- Sauna, massage, physical therapy procedures.

Friday: Improvement of the throwing technique, development of speed and movement coordination capacities. Training means:

- Acrobatics exercises

- Starts, accelerations and specific speed exercises (different starts, sudden direction changes).

- Throwing of the javelin and light implements.

- Imitation exercises.

- Standing jumps, long, triple and high jumps from a runup.

Saturday: Development of the power capacities of the delivery movements, development of strength and jumping capacities. Training means:

- Throwing of the javelin and other implements.

- Complex weight training exercises.

- Long, triple and high jumps (standing and from a runup), gymnastics exercises (high bar).

Sunday: Rest.

A SAMPLE DAY

The principle of a weekly cycle is used in training processes for the development of the functional capacities of javelin throwers, as well as in movement-emphasized manner during the pre-competition period. The training volume in the development of functional capacities re-

mains virtually the same for all athletes during the winter preparation period. However, the intensity (weight of the different implements, distances thrown, etc.) is adjusted individually.

A typical day"s training during this period is made up of the following activities:

Morning—Warmup, general exercises on the wall bars and the high bar (15 min), 6 x 40 to 50m sprints.
- Specific exercises with a 700g javelin, including flexibility exercises, standing target throws from head level (10 reps), standing throws into the net with a full arm action (10 reps), throws from a 3- to 5-stride runup (10 reps), throws from the transition strides (15 reps), final delivery imitation exercises.
- 5 x 50m sprints with the javelin, high bar exercises (2 x 5 reps of upstarts, 2 x 8 reps of pullups), 250m jog.

- Total training time: 100 to 105 minutes.

Afternoon—Warmup, general exercises on the wall bars (10 to 12 min).
- Complex exercises with shots of different weights, including two-handed backwards over the head (10 reps), two-handed forward-upward (10 reps) throws (7.26kg), hand-to-hand shot handling exercises, sideways throws (6kg), forward throws without using the legs and trunk (all these 2 x 5 reps).

- Depth jumps, upward jumps (70 to 80cm), javelin runups (3 x 30m), abdominal and back exercises with 15 to 20kg weights (4 x 10 reps), bounding on the spot (200 reps).

- Total training time: 135 minutes.

The number of throws is gradually increased as the spring approaches and eventually reaches 200 to 250. There is also more variety in the weight of the implements (shots, stones, balls), which are thrown from various positions for the development of explosive power in the final delivery action.

These throws make up about 25% of the total time during the winter period. The yearly volume reaches 9000 throws, of which 8000 throws are one-handed (with 900, 800 and 700g javelins, 2 to 3kg shots and 100 to 1000g stones and balls).

All these throws should be executed according to biomechanical principles, and athletes have to learn the movement coordination of the basic throws. Coaches should regularly control the quality of the throws, even when dealing with high-level performers. A "throw as you like" approach is unacceptable, as the task of the exercises is to adapt the involved muscle groups and joints gradually to the specific power and strength demands of the javelin delivery.

TABLE 1: THE TRAINING OF OVTSHINIKOV DECEMBER 1, 1988 TO MARCH 1, 1989.

TRAINING EXERCISES	MONTHS			
	DEC	JAN	FEB	TOTAL

Javelin throw (number of throws)
    Normal javelin
    Heavier javelin (900g)
	—
	380
		50
		322
			205
			125
				255
				827

Two-handed throws of different weights (4-16kg)	850	1104	946	2900
One-handed throws of different implements (100-3000g)	110	296	258	664
Jumps (standing, runup, depth, upward, multiple)	800	1000	800	2600
Running with the javelin (m)	2000	2000	1600	5600
Weight training (tonnes)	62	75	56	192

THE YEAR'S PLAN

The training plan of a year is adjusted to the demands made by the competition calendar and is divided into periods of six to eight weekly microcycles with the following basic tasks:

November - December: Emphasis is on strength and power development, combined with the improvement of technical elements.

January - February: The improvement of the javelin throw as a whole is added to the tasks of the previous period.

March - April: Emphasis is mainly on development of speed capacities. Our athletes perform a large volume of exercises that help to develop these capacities (throwing of lighter implements, throwing the javelin, sprinting, jumping and bounding).

May - June: Preparation for the main competitions (participation in three to four minor competitions). Emphasis is on throwing the basic implements, development of power and strength and psychological preparations.

July - August: The main competitions of the season. Because competitions take place virtually every week, the total training load volume is reduced by about 30% compared to the previous period. However, the high intensity level of the maintenance of power is continued. Throws with normal-weight javelins make up 70% of the volume, throws with lighter implements 30%. More attention is paid to restoration procedures after the competitions.

September - October: Participation in late-season competitions, followed by active rest, rehabilitation and general physical activities.

An example of the work performed in the preparation period is summed up in Table 1. It shows Ovchinnikov's training during 1988-89 (December - March). As can be seen, the largest workload occurs in January. The load drops in February before the USSR winter championships, although the number of throws with the competition javelin continues to increase.

We use specific exercises as control tests to monitor and to evaluate the power development of javelin throwers. These well-known tests take place every two months and are comprised of the following exercises:

1. The two-handed shot thrown backward over the head (m).
2. The two-handed shot thrown from behind the neck from a runup (m).
3. The standing triple jump (m).
4. The snatch (barbell) (kg).

The results of such control tests are shown in Table 2. Considering that we are dealing with 18- to 19-year-old javelin throwers, the results are completely satisfying.

TABLE 2: CONTROL TESTS RESULTS OF FOUR JAVELIN THROWERS IN 1988 AND 1989.

ATHLETE	TEST NO. 1		TEST NO. 2		TEST NO. 3		TEST NO. 4	
	1988	1989	1988	1989	1988	1989	1988	1989
MALE: VO AC	(7.25 kg) 17.82 17.20	 18.18 17.55	(4 kg) 20.60 21.40	 20.00 21.70	 8.96 8.84	 9.16 9.00	 90 100	 95 100
FEMALE: OT TM	(4 kg) 15.85 15.15	 16.70 16.20	(3 kg) 15.30 14.80	 15.80 14.96	 — 6.90	 7.76 7.06	 52.5 50	 57.5 52.5

TRENDS IN JAVELIN CONDITIONING

by Jimmy Pedemonte, Italy

Italian throwing coach Jimmy Pedemonte discusses contemporary trends in the physical conditioning of javelin throwers, with reference to selected examples of methods employed in different European countries.

Javelin throwing belongs to a group of events in which in a short time a change of the biokinetic chain takes place, with an immediate increase of the effort in the final part. These technical exigencies require good special physical preparation and, also, a high level of coordination that can influence the mechanisms governing the movements and enable full exploitation of the potential strength.

Consequently, it is necessary to establish an optimal combination of training methods that can improve the level of development and the quality of the movements. Particularly important are the training methods characterized by the increase (in volume and intensity) of the special components of training. Many Soviet and other foreign authors are convinced that the real heart of the matter is to establish methods and means that lead to a balance between the improvement of explosive strength and development of the technical movements.

Trends toward methods aimed at the indiscriminate increase of training volume and intensity do not lead to effective results. This is the reason why, in theory and in practice, several different methods exist. Many athletes use low or medium loads, executed quickly or with medium speed. Some use medium loads until failure, while others use high loads, up to 85-95% of their maximum, taking care that there are favorable conditions for neural coordination. As it often happens, the truth lies in the middle.

Today it is held that a change in the weight training loads is the best way to improve explosive strength. The Soviet physiologist Golinievsky claims that we can change the nature of stimuli (mechanical, chemical, physical) but this change is not perceived by the organism that reacts to a change in intensity of stimuli. In explosive events, like the javelin throw, the most utilized methods are therefore based on fast movements, circuit training, concentric and eccentric contractions, and the like.

However, the most effective way to improve explosive strength is to use the varied method, that is, to use exercises characterized by different types of muscular tensions. The variation of methods can follow a wavelike course or a sharp, clean change in the succession of loads applied during the various stages of the yearly training cycle.

In the Soviet Union, elite javelin throwers widely use methods that incorporate high-, medium- and low-intensity training loads. This training system, because of its frequent changes, avoids the negative reaction of an organism to repeated, stereotyped stimuli and increases the organism's efficiency.

STRENGTH AND TECHNIQUE

In events like the javelin the problem of increasing explosive strength is successfully solved through the improvement of strength, because strength leads to an increase of speed against resistance. This correlation is explained by the physiological connection between the development of strength and speed.

The same principle is true when training with light and heavy implements. A monotonous use of light and heavy implements during the various stages of training can lead to a unilateral development detrimental to the basic technical model.

An investigation to determine the best methods for improvement of strength should be directed to the attainment of a balance between strength improvement and the betterment of the technical components of the performance. In other words, the objective is to build up a functional mutual cooperation between technique and strength, so that technique is developed on a positive and favorable functional basis.

Dmitrussenko has undertaken important research on this topic. In the past, Soviet javelin throwers used loads close to 80% of maximum, with 7-8 repetitions in each set, during the preparation period (from November to April). During the competition period (from May to September), they moved to higher intensities, up to 95%, with 2-3 repetitions in each set. From experience with this program, they deduced that during the preparation period strength improved because of an adaptation to a vegetative type medium intensity load that enhances the increase of muscular mass.

During the competition period, when submaximal intensities were used, strength improved because of a better nervous regulation—that is, a recruitment of more motor units that were better synchronized. So, different methods correspond to different contributions to improved strength.

In accordance with this principle it has been established that the alternation of a series of methods can lead to a more optimal development of strength in relation to javelin throwing. This method is called the "mixed method."

An experiment was conducted on two groups of javelin throwers, where the control group followed the traditional method and the other group the mixed method. The experiment was verified through 60 tests, among them standing throws with implements of different weights, the speed of the throwing arm without any resistance, the strength of the fundamental muscular groups, the deviations from the technical model, the time of the runup according to the change of weight of the implements and, of course, the standard throw at full effort.

The results showed that training with low intensities must be done during the first part of the preparation period, when the aim is to increase the muscle mass and when the athlete trains twice a day.

The experiment also indicated that high-intensity loads must be exactly programmed, otherwise results could be negative. Therefore, high-intensity strength training in the morning and technical work in the evening is considered inefficacious and detrimental to technical progress.

On the other hand, the mixed method has led to a great increase of static and dynamic strength, especially after a 24-hour recovery. It is important to point out that the frequent change of methods typical of the mixed system doesn't negatively influence the temporal and rhythmical organization of the runup.

Of course, there are also problems concerning the development of specific throwing strength. On this topic investigations are conducted all over the world. Experts try to pick out specific exercises with weights that reproduce the structure of the competitive movement and its dynamical character. Throwing implements of different weights is included in this.

In the Soviet Union, specific exercises are, above all, used according to the mixed method, within a single session, or during a group of sessions. In the first case, they avail themselves of the delayed effect of training because of the previous weight training (cumulative effect). In the second case, the development of technical movements is connected with blocks of speed or strength.

It is very interesting to note that the Soviets also use the isometric method for the improvement of release speed. They use exercises performed at full intensity for 1.0-2.0 seconds. These skills improve explosiveness and the capacity of relaxation of the muscles.

EUROPEAN INFORMATION

Now to some additional information on the conditioning of javelin throwers in European countries.

West Germans include speed training sessions in the program two to three times a week. One of these workouts includes running drills with the javelin. Several drills are performed in the beginning of the preparation period because running technique improves the runup with the javelin. The runs are usually over 30 to 60m and 100m.

During the competition period, each sprint is timed. Top German javelin throwers run 30m in 3.5 to 3.7 sec. and some are capable of running the 100m in less than 11 sec. In spite of this, they still work on the development of speed. Once a week, for the entire year, sprints over 30m or farther are performed, the first half with the javelin forward and the second half with the javelin drawn back.

Another important element for the improvement of speed is jumping training. Two to three weekly units are scheduled with 80 to 90 jumps each. Starting in February, jumps become more intense—for example, jumps from double-leg takeoffs over 1.06m hurdles. Tafelmeier had a best mark of 21.50 in the five hops from a three-stride runup and reached over 7m in the long jump.

Among strength training exercises, West Germans consider the snatch, jerk, squat, stepup and clean as basic. Wessing and Schreiber prefer front squats, while Wolfermann used to do parallel squats. The pullover is considered to be a specific-strength drill. Wessing had a pullover best of 95kg.

From October to February, strength training is repeated two or three times a week. Between 6 and 10 reps are performed in sets of 4 to 6 for 6 to 8 weeks. Then they gradually move to more intense weights: 4 to 6 sets of 3 to 5 reps at about 90%.

During the competition period, the intensity is changed. Instead of heavy weights, the German javelin throwers use a system of 6 to 8 reps of 60% to 70% at maximum speed. Heavy implements are used especially from November to the first half of January. The implements used include 1 to 4kg shots, with standing throw up to 28 meters.

Medicine balls, weighing from 2 to 5kg, are thrown up to four times a week. This is alternated with single throws of a heavy javelin or shot, followed by two double-arm throws of a medicine ball.

In Hungary, strength training is carried out with the use of pyramids. The country's throwers usually perform 6 to 7 sets increasing and decreasing the load. They basically use a reduced load with a high frequency of movements.

Former West German thrower Michael Wessing.

In the Soviet Union, javelin throwers follow the periodization concepts used by hammer throwers, but there are some differences. Since a great number of throws is considered dangerous to the elbow, they begin to throw later. They usually start in January, but all-out efforts are employed starting in May.

The use of axes takes place three times a week, employing 300 to 400 chopping movements with one or both hands. The axe weighs no more than 2.5kg and has a 100cm long handle. Other exercises consist mainly of medicine ball throws from different positions.

Starting in January, one-handed throws are included. In February they use the standard javelin, in March a heavy bar (pole) up to 1.1kg in weight. In April the 700g javelin, in May the standard and the women's javelin.

Soviet throwers avoid the practice of throwing javelins of different weights in the same session because it hinders the rhythm of the action. They prefer to throw only the 600g javelin for two or three weeks in order to avoid the formation of a stereotyped action. Just as sprinters use downhill sprints for breaking the speed barrier, top throwers use light javelins for breaking the specific throwing speed barrier.

In Italy, training to build up overall strength begins with the execution of a limited number of what are called fundamental exercises, including bench press, squats and similar lifts. Strength training with a large number of "com-plimentary" exercises is gradually reduced so as to move on to the fundamental exercises. We train all muscular groups, including those not directly recruited in the throwing action itself, with a large number of repetitions.

The fundamental exercises are compound drills; they require the participation of several groups of muscles—for instance, in the bench press the pectorals, frontal deltoids and triceps.

We feel that to obtain better performance in these basic exercises, it is necessary to start with complementary exercises, which are isolation drills. After switching over to the fundamental exercises, all the individual muscle groups that take part in these movements are already sufficiently strengthened and thus able to make a greater contribution to the economy of the compound movement.

As the Soviets do, we in Italy have a winter outdoor national championship, preceded by a couple of other outdoor competitions for the discus, hammer and javelin throw. This allows us to follow the new cycling method in which technical work is pursued all year long.

I have divided the preparation into two-month cycles. During each cycle the percentage of general, specific and technical preparation is gradually changed, according to the principle of "qualitative gradualness." The sequence of dominant elements have been scheduled as: general - specific - transformation - competition.

GENERAL AND SPECIFIC EXERCISES FOR JAVELIN THROWERS

by A. Stasjuk, Russia

The author looks at some common technical faults observable among javelin throwers and presents a series of general and specific exercises aimed at improving technical efficiency.

It wasn't so long age that the new javelin was introduced, yet distances reached by some top level performers are already very close to the 100-meter barrier. These obvious improvements indicate a better biomechanical approach to the development of javelin technique as well as a better understanding of the training means by which specific physical performance capacities are developed.

Nevertheless, many athletes—including some elite performers—allow themselves to be restricted by basic technical shortcomings. Some of these include:

- A final delivery action that is directed slightly across the axis of the javelin.
- An overbending of the knee joint of the left leg (of right-handed throwers) in the final delivery phase that leads to an increased release angle and an increased angle of attack.
- A lack of an active transfer from the runup to the final throwing stride. From the contemporary technical viewpoint, there should be an uninterrupted forward movement of the athlete's center of gravity from the start of the runup to the final positioning of the left leg for the delivery.

RECOMMENDED EXERCISES

Group 1—These exercises aim to prepare and develop the muscle groups involved in the forward movement action of the trunk and shoulder girdle.

Advisory remarks:
a) The inside of the shoulder blade should be compressed, the chin lifted and the trunk slightly bent in the initial position of all Group I exercises;
b) the movement of the trunk in the horizontal plane should be abruptly broken in Exercises 1 and 2;
c) the movement of the trunk in the vertical plane should be abruptly broken in Exercises 3 to 7.

The exercises are performed in three to five series of 20 to 50 repetitions.

Group II—These exercises aim to develop the forward movement of the hips, the fixation of the knee joint angle of the right leg, and the creation of tension in the left leg. The exercises, using single- or double-handed throws, are performed with loads ranging from 3.0 to 7.25kg.

Advisory remarks:
a) Exercises 10 to 13 are performed in a single-support position;
b) in Exercise 8 the forward bend of the trunk should take place without an extension of the legs;
c) the shoulders should not be turned to the left in Exercise 9;
d) in all the exercises the lower leg and ankle flexors are actively working, while the angle between the hip and the lower leg is maintained.

Group III—These exercises aim to develop the athlete's ability to apply exertion in the direction of the axis of the implement.

Advisory remarks:
a) Exercise 18 is performed with the feet placed parallel, throwing into the ground (10 to 15m);
b) Exercise 19 is performed from a wide throwing stance, Exercise 20 from a closer stance with a 25 to 30° release angle;
c) it is important that Exercises 19 and 20 are performed from a correct starting position, with the left elbow moving backward-downward and the right elbow below the implement.

The exercises are performed in two to three series of 10 repetitions.

Group IV—These exercises aim to develop an effective throwing stride for the final delivery action. Most important here is an active and smooth transfer from the transition stride into the throwing stride.

Advisory remarks:
a) Exercise 21 is performed slowly with static (three to five sec) starting and final positions;
b) Exercise 22 is executed from a three-stride approach in which the first stride represents a left leg swing from the hip and the left shoulder continues to move forward during all three strides;
c) Exercise 23 is executed from a four-stride walk, Exercise 24 from four to six running strides.

Group V—The exercises aim to develop the javelin runup, stressing the coordination of the forces applied in the work of the left and right legs.

Advisory remarks:
a) The axis of the shoulders and the javelin must in all exercises remain parallel;
b) vertical fluctuation of the body's center of gravity should be kept to a minimum;
c) running with the javelin in Exercise 25 must take place without turning the trunk to the right;
d) emphasis in Exercise 27 is placed on the left leg action, in Exercise 28 on the right leg action;
e) emphasis in Exercise 29 is placed on a smooth combination of the left leg swing and the right leg drive.
The exercises are performed in two to three series of 50 to 100m.

Group VI—General preparation exercises.

Advisory remarks:

a) Exercise 30—walking with a bar on the shoulders;
b) Exercise 31—forward and backward leg movements against the resistance of a rubber band while holding onto a wall ladder;
c) Exercise 32—development of groin flexibility and strength;
d) Exercise 33—knee bends in the delivery position;
e) Exercise 34—sideways bends with a weight disc;
f) Exercise 35—development of lower leg strength on a gymnastics horse while holding onto a wall ladder;
g) Exercise 36—same as Exercise 35 in a different direction;
h) Exercise 37—above the head pulls in a prone position to develop the trunk flexors (resistance 50 to 100kg);
i) Exercise 38—performance of the transition stride (cross stride) from a standing position onto a lower surface without changing the pre-delivery position;
j) Exercise 39—same as Exercise 38 from a three-stride approach;
k) Exercise 40—bounding with an emphasis on maintaining static tension in each landing (three to four series of 20 to 25 takeoffs).
All exercises in this group except Exercise 40 can be performed in three to five series of 10 up to 20 repetitions.

THE JAVELIN RUNUP

by Hans Torim, Estonia

A detailed outline of the author's views on the javelin runup, from the initial stages to the impulse stride and the pre-delivery position.

THE INITIAL STAGE

At the start of the runup, the javelin is carried above the shoulder with the arm bent at the elbow and the hand holding the javelin about the height of the head. Slight differences in this position depend on individual preferences for the withdrawal action.

The runup is started from a check mark with the left foot forward, or a few preliminary walking or slow running strides before the left foot hits the check mark. The runup begins with a smooth acceleration and aims to reach in 8 to 10 running strides a movement speed that corresponds to the thrower's capacities and technical level. The final speed must allow the thrower to be ready for the beginning of the actual delivery.

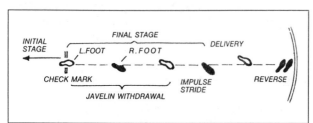

FIGURE 1: THE MAIN PHASES OF THE JAVELIN RUNUP

It is held that a suitable runup speed is about two-thirds of the maximal sprinting speed. Leading male throwers reach speeds of 7 to 8m/sec, female throwers 6 to 7m/sec.

Running is performed on the balls of the feet, avoiding bouncing or stamping on the spot. Shortening or lengthening of the strides in order to reach the final check mark is inefficient because the thrower must be psychologically and physically prepared for an optimal and relaxed withdrawal of the javelin, the impulse stride and the delivery.

This preparedness is fostered by performing the last strides of the initial stage with the help of inertia and without losses in forward speed.

THE FINAL STAGE

The final stage of the runup begins when the left foot hits the second check mark. The most common, simple and effective technique is the three-stride variation—two strides for the withdrawal of the javelin and one impulse stride (see Figure 2). All these strides are running strides, whereas the fourth stride should be included in the delivery phase.

The delivery stride, in contrast to the task of forward movement of the other strides, is involved in breaking the forward movement of the legs and hips. It is also not a running stride because the flight phase is missing.

FIGURE 2: THE IMPULSE STRIDE

The departure from the inclusion of the throwing stride with the runup allows for a better understanding in the analysis of the different movement phases of the javelin throw. Although the final stage of the runup and the delivery are closely connected, the above-described terminology, replacing what is normally referred to as a four-stride runup, appears to be justified.

Withdrawal Strides

The javelin withdrawal strides begin with the rotation

of the shoulder girdle to the right. It occurs smoothly without interrupting the forward progress of the body. While a slightly lifted left shoulder turns towards the runup direction, an active withdrawal of the throwing arm is still delayed. The athlete looks into the direction of the throw and there is no rotation in the hip girdle. The hip girdle is kept across the running direction, assisted by the forward drive of the right thigh.

There is a slight trunk rotation and, as the right leg lands after the flight phase, also some hip rotation. The right foot lands on its outside edge but remains pointed towards the running direction. The thrower continues the run with the legs and hips driving vigorously forward.

The withdrawal of the javelin is concluded in the second stride. It occurs smoothly and with a somewhat delayed action. The hand moves directly back to about ear level, and the javelin is kept close to the head. In this relatively ample and ground-covering running stride, the active legs and the hip girdle appear to "run away" from the throwing arm and shoulder, pulling the elbow joint straight.

A noticeable backward lean opposite to the throwing direction is created. From this stage on, the thrower appears to drag the javelin with straight but relaxed arm and throwing shoulder muscles. This "dragging" behind action and an optimal backward lean must continue until the delivery begins. The last will only succeed when the thrower can maintain relatively more active forward movement speed of the legs and hips compared to that of the arm and the throwing shoulder.

The "dragging" action can be disrupted when the forward movement of the legs and the hip girdle slows down, when the thrower delays the placement of the left leg in the throwing position, or when the arm is prematurely bent in the elbow. In this case the javelin and the arm "catch up" with the thrower, the backward lean is reduced, tension in the arm slackens, and the delivery movement is shortened.

A noticeable hip rotation takes place during the second withdrawal stride when the left leg makes an extensive forward movement. Some throwers at this moment even reach a position where the hip and shoulder axis are virtually parallel. This brings the thrower into a position where the trunk, the throwing arm and the javelin are close to what is required in the following pre-delivery position.

Some throwers do not complete withdrawal of the javelin at the end of the second stride (evidently for psychological reasons). They are not yet ready for the impulse stride and the following delivery, and so perform two supplementary strides, continuing to run with the hips and shoulders rotated to the right.

In this position it is rather difficult to maintain forward speed and a correct position of the trunk, shoulders and the throwing arm. For this reason a six-stride variation can not be recommended, particularly to beginners.

Impulse Stride

The impulse stride begins with an active placement of the left foot, transferred immediately into a sharp forward drive. The athlete pushes back against the track, moving the hip girdle actively forward. The right leg executes at the same time a fast movement directly forward that assists in shifting the thrower's body weight more quickly over the takeoff leg.

The takeoff into the impulse stride therefore takes place through an active gathering of widely split legs (thighs) in the flight phase of the previous stride, followed immediately by a forward-directed drive. The thrower now performs during a low, close to the track, flight phase an opposite-direction scissors movement, pushing the right foot actively down to simultaneously bring the left leg quickly forward. The left leg passes the right already during the flight and is considerably ahead of it at the moment the landing in the impulse stride has taken place.

Because the left leg has already passed the right, and because the right is placed on the track with an active downward-backward motion after the impulse stride, the right leg lands relatively close to the body's center of gravity. This allows the thrower to reach the delivery phase faster and with less loss of movement speed.

This is the reason why it is unnecessary to attempt to place the right leg as far as possible ahead of the body during the impulse stride. A long, and therefore high and breaking, impulse stride in order to get the legs further ahead of the body should consequently be avoided.

The right leg lands straight in the direction of the runup with an optimal knee bend and pre-tensed muscle. This enables avoidance of an overly deep bend in the knee joint when the body weight passes over it. The foot is more or less turned to the right of the throwing direction (45 to 90°), depending on the degree of hip rotation during the impulse stride.

The thrower strives during the impulse stride to maintain a relaxed position without muscular tension in the throwing arm, trunk and shoulder girdle. The head and the eyes are turned in the direction of the throw. Attention is directed to leg action and concentration to an undelayed beginning of the delivery phase.

There is an increased backward lean of the body when the right leg lands at the end of the impulse stride, due to the relatively more active forward movement of the legs and hips.

The actual moment of the landing of the right foot at the end of the impulse stride can be regarded as the kinematic dividing line between the runup and the delivery phases. The position of the thrower at this moment can therefore be regarded as the pre-delivery position.

The Pre-delivery Position

An efficient pre-delivery position following the impulse stride has the following characteristics:

- An optimal backward lean of the body (30 to 35°) with the left shoulder pointing in the throwing direction.

- The eyes looking slightly upward in the throwing

direction (30 to 35° upward-forward).

- The throwing arm, shoulder and elbow are extended back, opposite to the throwing direction, with the hand about ear level.

- The left arm, bent at the elbow, is placed about shoulder height.

- The front end of the javelin is held close to the head, approximately level with the eyes.

- The three axes (javelin, shoulder, hip) are virtually parallel to the direction of the throw. (The hip girdle can be turned somewhat less to the right).

- The foot of the right leg, pre-tensed and with an optimal knee bend, is turned 45 to 90° to the right of the throwing direction.

- A virtually straight left leg is already ahead of the right in the direction of the throw.

- There is no tension in the trunk, shoulder and the throwing arm muscles.

- The thrower is maximally prepared for the following delivery.

It should be noted that some variations can occur in the parameters of the pre-delivery position, depending on such specific individual features of a thrower as the runup speed, physical performance capacities, natural throwing action, and the control and understanding of technique.

However, these variations should not exceed certain optimal limits, nor be contrary to the biomechanical principles of the technique. As these same "rules" apply to the following delivery phase, it is essential that the pre-delivery position is favorable for an effective delivery. The lightning fast delivery does not allow sufficient time for corrections.

The javelin runup can be summed up as follows:

RUNUP PHASES	
INITIAL STAGE	**FINAL STAGE**
About 6 to 12 running strides	Javelin withdrawal Two strides + impulse stride
Begin: Basic position	Begin: First withdrawal stride
End: Start of the withdrawal (Reaching the check mark)	End: Landing of the right foot after the impulse stride (Pre-delivery position)
Main task: Development of maximal speed for the athlete-javelin system. Preparedness for the following actions.	Main task: Maintenance of the speed of the athlete-javelin system. Reaching an optimal pre-delivery position.

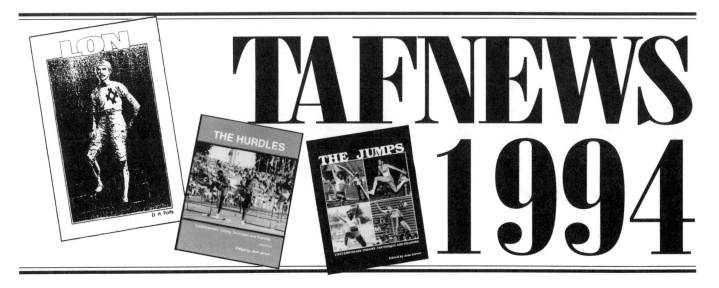